AF518015

THE ROLE OF THE STATE IN SOUTH ASIA AND OTHER ESSAYS

Perspecitves in History

General Editors
B.N. Goswamy
Ravinder Kumar
Dietmar Rothermund

Vol. I. Dietmar Rothermund: *Asian Trade and European Expansion in the Age of Mercantilism.*

Vol. II. Dietmar Rothermund: *The Indian Economy Under British Rule and other Essays.*

Vol. III. Kapil Kumar: *Peasants in Revolt: Tenants, Landlords, Congress and the Raj in Oudh, 1886-1992.*

Vol. IV. Ravinder Kumar: *The Making of a Nation: Essays in Indian History and Politics.*

Vol. V. Dietmar Rothermund: *Mahatma Gandhi: An Essay in Political Biography.*

Vol. VI. Dietmar Rothermund: *India in the Great Depression, 1929-1939.*

Vol. VII. Hermann Kulke: *Kings and Cults: State Formation and Legitimation in India and Southeast Asia.*

Vol. VIII. Dietmar Rothermund: *The Role of the State in South Asia and Other Essays.*

The Role of the State in South Asia and Other Essays

DIETMAR ROTHERMUND

MANOHAR
2000

First published 2000

© Dietmar Rothermund, 2000

All rights reserved. No part of this publication may be reproduced or transmitted, in any form or by any means, without the prior permission of the author and the publisher

ISBN 81-7304-361-2

Published by
Ajay Kumar Jain for
Manohar Publishers & Distributors
4753/23 Ansari Road, Daryaganj
New Delhi 110002

Printed at
Rajkamal Electric Press
B 35/9 GT Karnal Road Indl. Area
Delhi 110033

CONTENTS

PREFACE

Forty years ago I first landed in India after a slow voyage on board a freighter. After a *Bharat Darshan* I settled down in New Delhi and worked at the National Archives, collecting material for my book on the Indian freedom movement. This movement had inspired me when I was still in school. I had experienced Nazi rule which I instinctively found to be repulsive. The ideas of Gandhi and Nehru were more appealing to me. I read Nehru's autobiography and wrote a letter to him to which I got no reply at that time. Of course, he had more important things to do than to reply to the letter of a German teenager. But I decided that one day I would surely ask him the questions which I had put to him in my letter. I got this chance in two long interviews in January 1961.

My attachment to India and my work in Indian history has continued ever since. The present volume of essays is a small sample of my recent studies. The text of the first essay was originally the manuscript of a lecture which I delivered at Charles University, Prague, in September 1998. It was the inaugural lecture of the 15th European Conference on Modern South Asian Studies. I had been associated with these conferences since their inception in the late 1960s and I felt honoured by the invitation of Charles University which celebrated its 650th anniversary in 1998. I am particularly grateful to Professor Jaroslav Vaček, Director of the Institute of Indian Studies, in this context. The present essay is a revised and enlarged version of the Prague lecture. But I have retained the style of the lecture rather than converting the text into a learned paper with many footnotes.

The subsequent paper was originally a contribution (in German) to a volume dealing with the market and state power in history (H. Breuninger/R. P. Sieferle, eds., *Markt und Macht in der Geschichte*, Stuttgart 1995). I abbreviated the text as I had to eliminate passages which would appear repetitive in the context of the present volume. Nevertheless, some repetitions have remained in the text as it would have otherwise appeared somewhat disjointed.

The third essay on "Town and Country in India" was initially contributed to a *Festschrift* for my colleague and friend Niels Steensgaard (J. Johansen/E. Petersen/H. Stevnsborg, eds., *Clashes of Cultures. Essays in Honour of Niels Steensgaard*, Odense 1992) The editors suggested to me that I should write about "town and country" and I tried my best to rise to the occasion. Again I had to eliminate some passages from the original text so as to avoid repetition.

The fourth essay was originally published in German. A political academy of the German army had asked me for a lecture on security issues concerning India. Subsequently I was asked by the editor of the Austrian yearbook on international security to submit this manuscript for publication (Erich Reiter, ed., *Österreichisches Jahrbuch für internationale Sicherheitspolitik*, Graz 1997). Like all comments on current affairs this paper appears to be dated as it was written before India and Pakistan embarked on their nuclear tests. In my assessment I was influenced by the benign Gujral Doctrine at that time, but as I hope that India may in due course return to that wise statesman's policy, I did not change the arguments I presented. Moreover, the paper also contains my comments on Samuel Huntington's pernicious theory of the "Clash of Civilisations" and I still adhere to my views expressed in this context.

The fifth paper was written in English for the German journal *ASIEN* (No. 68/1998). I reproduce it here with only minor omissions. As it was addressed to readers who are not necessarily familiar with Indian politics I had to add some information which may appear redundant to Indian readers. Some remarks on "Future Perspectives" are outdated by now, but I have retained the perspective of 1998.

The sixth paper on "Individual and Group Rights in Western Europe and India" is the product of a challenge which I had to face when I was invited to a conference organised by the Konrad Adenauer Foundation at the beautiful Fort Neemrana in March 1999. My colleague and friend Dieter Conrad, a noted law scholar, had been asked to deal with this subject, but a sudden illness prevented him from attending the conference. Thus I had to step in and I did so with some trepidation as I am not a law scholar. However, when I delved into the relevant literature, I found the subject fascinating. I hope I have done justice to it. I am grateful to Dr. Helmut Reifeld for inviting me to this conference and permitting me to reproduce my paper here. It is also included in a volume edited by him on "Pluralism and Equality. Values in Indian Politics and Society" published by Sage, New Delhi. The publishers were so kind as to agree to this more or less simultaneous publication. I wish to recommend this volume edited by Dr. Reifeld to my readers. It reflects the spirit of the stimulating Neemrana conference.

In the seventh essay on "Nationalism and the Reconstruction of Traditions in Asia" I am returning to a theme which has interested me ever since I wrote my book on the Indian freedom movement. This paper was originally a contribution to a *Festschrift* for my colleague and friend Bernhard Dahm (S. Kuhnt-Saptodewo, V. Grabowsky, M. Großheim, eds., *Nationalism and Cultural Revival in Southeast Asia: Perspectives from the Centre and the Region,* Wiesbaden 1997). Professor Dahm was head of the Department of Southeast Asian Studies at Passau University. A paper restricted in its scope to South Asia only would not have done justice to this *Festschrift*, therefore I adopted a wider perspective. In doing so I had to venture into regions on which I have not done any research of my own. But I prepared the ground for a comparative approach by doing a joint seminar with experts in Chinese and Japanese studies at Heidelberg University on this subject in 1993.

The final essay on "Nation and Region in Indian Historiography" was originally the manuscript of a lecture presented at a conference on "The East and the Meaning of History" held in Rome in November 1992. The term "meaning of history" was actually a misleading translation of the Italian term "senso storico". The participants of the conference were not asked to find out about the meaning of history but had to deal with the historical awareness of different nations. Doing this for India was a tall order and I tried to cope with it by highlighting some issues which seemed of importance to me.

Heidelberg, January 2000 Dietmar Rothermund

1

THE ROLE OF THE STATE IN SOUTH ASIA

South Asia has given rise to many types of states in five millenia of an impressive history from the early states of the Indus civilisation to the present democracies of the subcontinent which encompass nearly a quarter of mankind. When Hegel and Schlegel debated the merits of ancient India in the early years of the 19th century not much was known about the origin of states in that part of the world. Therefore Hegel who thought of the state as the highest achievement of mankind tended to look down upon India (Halbfass 1988). India had obviously been unable to reach the goal of state formation even though it had produced marvels of ancient literature which were praised by Schlegel in his book on "The Language and Wisdom of the Indians". (Rothermund 1986) Hegel argued that even such marvels meant little if they were not accompanied by state formation. In the further course of the 19th century nationalist Indians tried hard to find traces in their history which would meet Hegel's criteria. Their British masters asserted that India's greatness manifested itself purely in the spiritual sphere and that it lacked the political skill required for state formation. The British, of course, liked to derive their right to rule over India from this assessment. While still denying this right, many Indian nationalists nevertheless acquiesced in the assessment that Indias glory consisted of spiritual rather than political excellence. Compensating for the lack of political power, they could adopt a "holier than thou"-attitude towards their foreign rulers. This changed to some extent after the re-discovery of Kautilya's "Arthashastra" in 1905, the same year in which the Japanese defeated Russia. While that victory fired the imagination of the Indian nationalists immediately, the reception of the "Arthashastra" took a little longer but had a much more lasting effect. This highly sophisticated treatise on statecraft demonstrated that India was well advanced in political thought and practice long before the British had acquired a state of their own.

The "Arthashastra" provides an interesting point of departure for discussing the role of the state in South Asia. Like most Brahminical texts it contains normative precepts rather than a description of historical facts. Moreover, it is supposed to have been composed for Chandragupta Maurya but reflects in its *Rajamandala* the experience of earlier states rather than that of the Maurya empire. These differences shall be explained later on. At this point it should only be noted that the "Arthashastra" is not consulted here as a historical source but for its interesting concept of the state. This concept is not expressed in terms of an explicit theory of the state. There is only one reference to the idea that the people asked a king to rule them so as to save them form the chaos of *matsyanyaya*, i.e. big fishes swallowing the smaller ones, the Indian version of Hobbes' *homo homine lupus*. Interestingly enough, Kautilya lets a secret agent propound this theory so as to enhance the loyalty of the people. Kautilya comments on this that it is useful if the people believe in such a theory, but in subsequent statements he provides evidence that he himself does not believe in it. His concept of the state is pragmatic and functional, he portrays it as a network of interrelated activities. He lists seven elements (*saptanga*) of the state: the king, the minister, the inhabited country, the fortress, the treasury, the army and the ally. The citizens or subjects of the king are subsumed under the term *janapada* (inhabited country). The minister (*amatya*) obviously stands for the royal administration in general. Mentioning the ally among the seven elements of the state, Kautilya contextualises the state. Whereas other political theorists would regard the state as a self-contained system, Kautilya thought of the state in terms of concentric circles both as far as internal as well as external relations were concerned. The ally provided the link between internal and external relations. We shall keep this idea in mind when analysing the various stages of state formation in South Asia.

The Puzzles of the Indus Civilisation

The earliest evidence of state formation in South Asia are the impressive cities of the Indus civilisation. When they were first discovered in the 1920s, it was held that they must have been colonies of the Mesopotamian civilisation. But subsequent explorations have shown that at some sites going back to the 6th millenium B.C. the precursors of the Indus civilisation were well advanced in the methods of settled agriculture. Moreover, the features of the material culture of the Indus region were quite distinct from that of Mesopotamia, they definitely showed a clear profile of indigenous development. The Indus civilisation obviously owed a great deal to the breeding of a special type of heat-resistant wheat (*Triticum aestivum sphaerococcum*) and to the domestication of a particular kind of cattle (*Bos indicus*). Later on it imported millets as well as cotton from East Africa, probably via Oman. The millets helped to extend the reach of the Indus civilisation to dry areas where wheat and barley could not grow. (Rissman & Chitalwala 1990). Cotton gave rise to textile production, some of this was exported to Mesopotamia where cotton was not yet grown at that time. It was only much later, around 700 B.C., when the Assyrian king Sennacherib tried to introduce the cultivation of Indian cotton at Nineveh. (Kuhrt 1995, Vol. II) Probably these attempts were due to the cessation of supplies from the Indus region which had earlier maintained a brisk trade with Mesopotamia. It is known that king Sargon I of Agade (Akkad) received ships from the Indus region around 2250 B.C. He even employed an interpreter of the Meluhha-language. (Kuhrt 1995, Vol. I) This may indicate that "Meluhha" was the name by which the citizens of the Indus civilisation referred to themselves. The word *mleccha* which means an impure stranger in later Indian languages may well have been derived from that name. The Meluhha-people must have survived even after their sophisticated political and social organisation had vanished. They probably appeared to be distinctively "strange" to newcomers.

The Indus civilisation must have supported well organised states, but as its script has not yet been deciphered, we have no information about the structure of those states. We may only derive some conclusions from the articulation of social spaces in the cities. There were no royal palaces or tombs. The citadels found in all major cities of this civilisation were obviously reserved for ritual functions and for a priestly class associated with those functions. This class may have exercised an oligarchic control. The amazing uniformity of weights and measures, the size of bricks etc. over a wide area seems to indicate such a control. The Indus civilisation did not know the horse and thus lacked the basic instrument for the rise of a specialised warrior class. The structure of the houses indicates that there was a kind of middle class of traders and cultivators, but also a working class of artisans. Two factors contributed to this kind of state formation. The first one was the need for organising agriculture in areas which were seasonally inundated by a mighty river. The Indus supplies twice as much water as the Nile when it is in spate. The second one was the organisation of a large volume of long distance trade. Priestly hegemony may have sufficed to keep this civilisation alive until ecological changes destroyed it. Such a hegemony may have been on the one hand a guarantee for the longevity of "empire" but on the other hand it was less flexible than the type of monarchy prevailing in neighbouring Mesopotamia. The history of the Mesopotamian civilisation is one of incessant warfare, but conquerors were always eager to consolidate their rule by integrating the areas which they had subjected by political as well as religious means. Resourceful monarchs could always make a new beginning, but the oligarchy which ruled in the region of the Indus civilisation was probably unable to cope with a dramatic change of the environmental conditions.

The puzzle of the political organisation of this vast agrarian "empire" could perhaps be solved if the script found on thousands of seals could be deciphered. However, even then we may not get much information about politics and religion as the short "texts" on the seals may refer to rather mundane matters and not to the structure of the state. On the majority of the seals the main symbol is that of a unicorn with the body of an ox. Its shoulders are invariably decorated with the same type of ornament which has the shape of a pack-saddle. It is thus highly likely that this symbol refers to a standardised load of grain. The different plant-like symbols in front of the animal may indicate the type of grain. The short "text" which accompanies these symbols may refer to the number of loads, and perhaps to the origin and/or destination of the goods. An Indian historian of science has recently made a plea for identifying the Indus script as numbers rather than letters (Subbarayappa 1996). His arguments sound plausible, but if he is right, the seals may only yield some information concerning the economic history of the "empire" but would still leave us in the dark about its political structure.

Kings, Sacrifices and Chariots: The Rise of the "Aryan" States

There was undoubtedly a hiatus between this type of state formation and the subsequent state formation of the people who referred to themselves as *Arya*. Recent Vedic research by Michael Witzel has demonstrated that the Kurus of Kurukshetra developed an idea of kingship which transcended the earlier forms of tribal leadership. (Witzel 1997) The Kuru kings consciously designed a "great tradition" so as to legitimise their rule. Witzel refers to this as a "first sanskritisation". Their public rituals were instruments of state formation. In thinking about the state we tend to have the modern state in mind and then describe early states in terms of what they lacked when compared to it. We should rather conceive of state formation as a strategy of stratification and incorporation. In this respect the Kuru kings seem to have been very creative. They camouflaged their innovations by adopting a consciously archaic articulation of their ideas. In this way they projected an ideal type of the early state which could then be reproduced elsewhere. Of course, once the magic of sacrifice in which the people believed in those times gave way to a different type of thought, the traditional features of these old states were only "cited" in a new environment. But the "state as citation" proved to be a powerful argument of political legitimation.

The chariot as the major instrument of warfare was intimately linked with early state formation, because it contributed to social stratification. The skills of the archer and his charioteer required specialised training. This led to the rise of a warrior elite. The empire of the Hittites in Western Asia (around 1400 B.C.) was ruled by kings who relied on such a warrior elite skilled in the use of chariots. These warriors were called *marianna* and the king had the right to select them. (Kuhrt 1995, Vol. I) It is possible that the *Arya* in India followed similar practices. The Vedic texts do not seem to shed much light on this. They do mention charioteers and give due importance to the makers of chariots who are visited by the king at the time of the great rituals. But there is no explicit reference to a group of warriors such as the *marianna*. Perhaps the "terrible" (*ugra*) warrior-companions of the Kuru kings had the same functions as the Hittite warriors.

The Kuru state was born in the beginning of the first millenium B.C. The model of this state with its king and its chariot-based elite soon spread throughout the North-Indian plains. Constant warfare among these states fostered the expansion of this type of state formation and also kept the warrior elites fit and aggressive. The means of domination available to each king were limited and thus the *janapada* which he could control was relatively small. Though a king had a circumscribed sphere of domination, he could have a much more extended potential of intervention. This was true even at this early stage. But chariots were not very well suited for long distance warfare. They were swift only on the battlefield. For transport over rugged terrain they had to be mounted on bullock carts and this severely limited their range of operation. The flexible test of sovereignty provided by the ritual of the horse-sacrifice (*ashvamedha*) was well adapted to this period of limited warfare. The horse selected for the sacrifice would roam freely for a year followed by the warriors of the respective king. If neighbouring kings did not obstruct its wanderings, they tacitly acknowledged the overrule of the king who had sent the horse, otherwise they had to fight and measure their strength against the challenger.

When this pastoral type of state formation was superseded by the growth of settled agriculture in the Gangetic plains there occurred what archaeologists have described as the second urbanisation of South Asia. Numerous sites have been discovered which permit the reconstruction of hierarchies of settlement. Capitals were surrounded at some distances by smaller towns. The capitals were heavily fortified. The city of Kausambi is an example of this new phase which began around the middle of the first millenium B.C. (Erdosy 1995) It is in this period that "the fortress", Kautilya's fourth element of the state, assumes great importance. It is significant that Kautilya does not mention the chariot-based warrior elite but refers in general terms to "the army". The norms which he abstracted from the experience of state-building and warfare in the Gangetic plains reflect the spirit of the period of the second urbanisation. The great empire which arose in the East in the fertile rice bowl of the lower Gangetic plains ushered in a totally different pattern of state formation.

The Empire of the East, the War-Elephant and the Spread of Buddhism

In Eastern India the rulers controlled a much larger domain and their potential of intervention was magnified by the use of the war-elephant. The chariot was no match for this new instrument of warfare. With the chariot the old warrior elite also went down. The archers on the elephant were to a large extent common soldiers and its guide was presumably a tribal from the forest in which it was caught. Elephants were not domesticated, they could only be tamed. Constant recourse to the forests which they inhabited was therefore essential for the rulers who wished to keep them. Otherwise they had to be bought for a high price. There was a virtuous circle conducive to empire building: the maintenance of trained war-elephants was expensive and only a mighty ruler could afford to keep them in adequate numbers, but such a ruler could then vanquish all smaller kings. Moreover, elephants could march long distances through rugged terrain, they thus extended the ruler's potential of intervention enormously. Chandragupta Maurya's gift of 500 elephants to Seleukos Nikator who then used them for his conquests in Western Asia is a striking example both of the size of such contingents and for the long distance which they could cover.

The Eastern empires also benefited from the access to iron ore which was in ample supply in the hills to the South of the Eastern plains. Tribal people in this area knew how to build furnaces with which they could convert this ore into a malleable metal. Weapons and instruments made of iron were useful for empire-building. The Nandas had practised this kind of empire-building before the Mauryas, but the latter perfected this type of the ancient Indian empire by adding new features to it.

Beyond sheer physical power and efficient organisation a state needs legitimation, or – to use Gramsci's term – it must establish a hegemony which assures the support or at least the acquiescence of the people. In the early states of the Gangetic plains this was achieved by the Brahmins who anointed the kings and impressed the people with their great Vedic sacrifices. The Eastern base of the new empires had never been sufficiently penetrated by the Brahmins. Moreover, new heterodox creeds had arisen in this region which challenged the relevance of the Brahminical ritual. The order of Buddhist monks had usurped the role of the Brahmins in the East. The name of the state of Bihar (Vihar= Buddhist monastery) signifies even today the impact of Buddhism on this region. It was in keeping with this background that Ashoka Maurya adopted Buddhism as a means to legitimise his imperial rule. It would be wrong to say that he made Buddhism a state religion. The concept of a state religion is anyhow alien to Indian thought. Moreover, the Buddhist creed was not at all state-oriented because it stressed individual salvation. Therefore it required a special ideological initiative to derive a message from Buddhism which could serve the purpose of legitimising imperial rule. Ashoka propagated in his edicts the ethics of benevolent hegemony aimed at the welfare of the people and peace. In one of his edicts he outlined in detail how he had qualified himself as a lay brother of the order of Buddhist monks. He obviously did this so as to show that he was entitled to control the discipline of the order. This was essential as he used Buddhist monks as emissaries to spread the message of his edicts. The text of the edicts was probably read out to the people at certain appointed times.

The enormous dimensions of Ashoka's empire were due to the fact that he faced no competitors and that he left many regions inhabited by unruly tribes to their own devices. Beyond the Eastern base of the empire he was mostly interested in controlling the routes of long distance trade from the coast of Kalinga to the mountains of the Northwest, and from the border of Nepal in the North to Karnataka in the South. The decline of this vast empire set in soon after Ashoka's death. Competitors came up who could emulate the strategies of imperial rule. Ashoka's peculiar adaptation of Buddhism as an instrument of legitimation was superseded by Brahminism once more. New empires like that of the Shatavahanas in the South revived ritual practices associated with the early kingdoms of the Gangetic plains although their states were very different from those early ones. When the mighty Shatavahana king celebrated a horse sacrifice, this was no longer connected with the flexible test of sovereignty mentioned above, but was meant to demonstrate that he was a great Hindu king following the precepts of ancient tradition. He was "citing" the model of the earlier state.

The acme of this development was the rise of the Gupta empire of Northern India. Its heartland was almost identical with that of the Maurya empire, but its structure was different from that of Ashoka's state. It faced more competitors. The Gupta rulers were great conquerors. In the central region of their empire they "uprooted" all rivals and introduced a well organised central administration. With their neighbours they maintained a balance of power occasionally accentuated by a demonstrative use of force such as Samudragupta's *digvijaya* (conquest of all quarters). It is signinficant that among the kings he subdued the mighty Vakatakas of Central India are conspicuous by their absence. His successor then established a marriage alliance with them and historians later on referred to the Vakataka-Gupta empire. This empire witnessed a flowering of urban culture, the spread of a monetised economy and an impressive literature. In analogy to the first period of sanskritisation mentioned by Witzel one may well refer to this as the second sanskritisation. Indologists usually concentrate on the literary achievements of this "Classical" age, but one should also take note of the political aspect of this sanskritisation. A royal style was articulated in this period which deeply influenced medieval state formation throughout the subcontinent and even beyond it in Southeast Asia.

The Structure of the Medieval State

After the Huns had wiped out the glory of ancient India, the model of the Gupta state was emulated by numerous regional kingdoms. The knowledge of statecraft and warfare was now more or less evenly spread and this prevented the rise of another great empire. Lalitaditya of Kashmir imitated once more Samudragupta's *digvijaya* but left no trace of his rule in those parts of India which he had traversed. Such type of conquest no longer had any imperial consequences. Regional kings determined the political style now, some of them expanded their realms occasionally, but in general one could speak of a balance of power. Kautilya's vision of the concentric state became once more appropriate for analysing this pattern of state formation. We had noted that in this concept the ally plays a crucial role in contextualising the state. Kautilya called the ally simply *mitra* (friend), but in medieval terminology we encounter the *samanta* (neighbour) who is initially outside the domain of the respective king, but becomes an insider when he joins the feudal hierarchy of the king. This process has been analysed in detail by Hermann Kulke. (Kulke 1995) Finally even the minister of the king could have the title of *mahasamanta.* This seems to be a paradoxical designation for the man who is at the very centre of royal power. But it is typical for a period when the *samantachakra,* the circle of subdued and incorporated neighbours, becomes the hallmark of the state.

In legitimising his position at the centre of the *samantachakra* the king had to stress his dynastic charisma. This he did by giving due importance to his genealogy. From the seventh century onward inscriptions and land grant documents on copper plates contain elaborate praise for the king's ancestors. (Chattopadhyaya 1995) The founder of the dynasty was often a local chieftain rather than a great king. Usually not much is said about him, but more detailed information is provided about the king's father and grandfather. In later periods the royal genealogists often try to trace the lineage of the king back to some mythical hero. Genealogical one-upmanship was necessary in the context of the *samantachakra*.

Burton Stein has introduced the term "segmentary state" into the discourse on state formation in India. (Stein 1995) It means that regional elements of the state are ruled by lords who reproduce the pattern of the king's rule on a smaller scale. The king exercises only ritual sovereignty over these lords. This concept does not do justice to the great weight of ritual sovereignty in pre-modern India and also neglects the pattern of cohesion and interaction among the elements of the state. Speaking of a "concentric state" is therefore more appropriate in the Indian context. This concept also helps to account for the "autonomous spaces" (Chattopadhyaya 1997) encircled by a state which does not aim at total territorial control, but tolerates local entities as long as they do not challenge the power of the state.

The concentric structure embodies both centripetal and centrifugal tendencies. It could happen that the *samantachakra* would keep even a weak dynasty going in order to serve their common interests. But, of course, *samantas* could also be tempted to go it alone or to join the *samantachakra* of a more powerful king. Invoking ritual sovereignty and thus making treason an offence against the god associated with the king was a powerful instrument for keeping *samantas* within the circle. Building an impressive temple in the centre of the realm would also attract donations from *samantas*. The great Brihadeshwara temple of the Cholas at Tanjore is a magnificent example of this type. It was soon matched by the Jagannath temple of Puri in Orissa. The great temple of Angkor Wat in Cambodia could also be mentioned in this context. It is interesting to note that the great cathedral of Speyer in Germany, the "imperial temple" of a mighty dynasty, was built at about the same time in the middle of the eleventh century as the Brihadeshwara temple.

Indian kings also adopted the wise stratagem of giving land grants to loyal Brahmins in the regions controlled by *samantas* who could not object to such pious donations. In this way the king could integrate his realm. In addition there was, of course, the prowess of the king demonstrated by long distance interventions. He could involve his *samantas* in such expeditions. In general there would hardly be any territorial gains, but there was fame and plunder which would richly reward all participants. Finally, there was the control of trade routes which interested medieval kings just as much as ancient empire builders.

Indian kingship of this type was an export article in great demand in Southeast Asia. It could be easily adapted to local conditions. Since Indian art and literature was an integral part of the manifestation of royal rule, it was also exported in this way. The sculptures depicting scenes of the Ramayana on the walls of the Prambanam temple in Indonesia are a testimony to the outreach of India's story-telling civilisation. The local adaptation is evident in the Javanese faces of the figures adorning the temple. The vision of the concentric state could thus radiate far beyond South Asia. The intimate connection of statecraft with religion, literature and the arts was the great achievement of medieval India.

The Sultanate as a Platform State

With the Islamic conquest a new type of state was superimposed on the medieval Hindu kingdom outlined before. Muslim conquerors had ventured into South Asia at an early date, but their rule had been limited to a part of the Indus valley. Mahmud of Ghazni had looted Northern India seventeen times in the early eleventh century, but he had not established his rule there. It was only in the early thirteenth century when the slave sultans of Delhi established their state that the whole of South Asia was subjected to a new type of state formation. The sultanate was a fairly new creation. The title sultan was first adopted by the Turk, Tögrilbeg, in 1040 AD. He had compelled the helpless Kalif to appoint him as his plenipotentiary (=*sultan*). Subsequently this title could be conferred by the Kalif on any ruler who was able and willing to legitimatise his rule in this way. Almost all sultans had the same sources of power: a cavalry manned by specially trained military slaves and supported by assignments (*iqta*) of land revenue. Military slavery was an avenue of rapid social advancement. Sultans were glad to rely on slaves who had no allodial ties and were supposed to be absolutely loyal to their lord. But as the example of the Delhi sultans shows, slaves could also cut the ties of allegiance to their lords. Moreover, sultanates rarely showed dynastic continuity, they were often ruled by one usurper after another. But even though there was no dynastic continuity, there was often a continuity of the state as such. Usurpers aimed at central power and not at carving out a territory of their own. Going it alone would have made them an easy prey for their erstwhile colleagues.

The swiftness of cavalry warfare greatly enhanced the potential of intervention over long distances. The Hindu kings who still managed to resist the power of the sultans were bound to copy their methods. They had to reorganise their states as cavalry states with the cavalry captain as the linchpin of local administration. Earlier organisations of local government were superseded in this way. A new type of urbanisation spread all over South Asia: the combined garrison and market town with the cavalry captain as head of both military and civil administration. The maintenance of the cavalry was extremely expensive, but the man on horseback was also a good revenue collector. Even the mere threat of cavalry intervention would make any peasant pay up his dues. Since the cavalry captain was usually a stranger in the area under his command and was also subject to transfer, he could not establish local ties and dare to rebel against his lord. Krishnadeva Raya, the greatest ruler of the Vijayanagar empire, was quite aware of the new state structure propagated by the Delhi sultanate and once referred to himself as a "Hindu sultan".

The new state structure had many negative features. First of all it created a gulf between urban and rural culture. The urban elite, mostly consisting of alien officers, drew its material sustenance from the countryside but kept aloof from its life, its language, its festivals. Since the urban centres were occupied by this new urban elite, they could not serve as focal points of local culture. Accordingly these urban centres more or less looked alike as they served the same military and administrative functions. The earlier concentric state was replaced by a platform state covering wide areas literally in a very superficial way. The platforms were decorated with a few impressive capitals but otherwise characterised by a rather barren uniformity.

The Modern Features of the Gunpowder Empire of the Great Mughals

The Mughal empire which was erected on the platform of the Delhi sultanate was in many respects an heir to its structure. It continued the practices of military feudalism based on revenue assignments to cavalry officers. By introducing the new field artillery and thus joining the ranks of the "gunpowder empires", the Great Mughals enhanced their central power. The sequence of the main strategic weapons from chariots to elephants to late medieval cavalry and finally to field artillery meant an ever increasing scale of military expenditure accompanied by the respective shifts in the concentration of power. Elephants and cavalry could still be matched by resourceful adversaries, but the field artillery was so expensive and required such skills in its deployment that it practically established a monopoly of power which could not be easily matched. The only challenge could emerge from guerilla warfare as that waged by Shivaji with his light cavalry or by rebellious peasants armed with primitive guns. Mughal edicts banning the possession of such weapons indicate that this must have been a real threat to their rule.

Maintaining Mughal rule required an efficient land revenue system and a collection of the revenue in cash rather than in kind. In a recent book on the financing of the English state from 1558 to 1714 Michael Braddick has called taxation and revenue collection "The Nerves of State". In England the taxation state evolved in the 16th century. From about 1650 to 1750 the extractive power of this state was greatly enhanced. The share of taxation in total national income rose from about 3 to 10 per cent in this period. Land tax and customs duties contributed about one third each to total revenue income. The land tax was assessed and collected by local commissions. Negotiation was built into the system and there was hardly any resistance. The Mughal state was much more dependent on land revenue which amounted to about 90 per cent of total taxation. The land revenue claim encompassed in general half of the agricultural produce. However, actual collection often fell short of this claim by about one third. The various intermediaries charged with the collection of revenue retained about 20 per cent of the amount collected. If one considers these intermediaries to be part of the Mughal state machinery, the state appropriated about one third of the agricultural produce. It is difficult to estimate the national product of Mughal India. The contribution of the large service sector encompassing the army is hard to gauge. But nevertheless agriculture can be safely assumed to be the most important sector of the Mughal economy. We may thus estimate that the Mughal state extracted at least a quarter of national income and was in this way even in the 16th century ahead of the English state of the 18th century.

Akbar, the greatest of the Great Mughals, had rationalised the land revenue system in a very effective way. In the early years of his rule he had still to follow the precedent set by his predecessors who had to fix the annual revenue rate themselves as it was an arbitrary decision. The expansion of his empire with its many regional differences made this decision even more arbitrary. He had, therefore, ordered a ten year statistical survey which took account of local price levels and different crops. The averages derived from these data could then be used for computing future revenue collections. The revenue authorities were also authorised to give credit (*taqavi*) calculated in terms of multiples of the annual revenue rate for the investment in improvements such as the building of wells. This institution exists even today, but since land revenue has dwindled, the credit which could be claimed in this way would be so insignificant that nobody would bother to apply for it. In Mughal times this type of credit was very important. The state was interested in enhancing the revenue paying capacity of the agriculturists in this way.

Akbar also rationalised the hierarchy of imperial officers by assigning ranks (*mansab*) to them which defined their salary as well as the contingent of cavalry which they had to maintain. The reorganised revenue system served as an ideal infrastructure of this imperial hierarchy. Revenue assignments could be accurately matched with the respective ranks. The system worked well as long as Akbar controlled it. His successors took its working for granted and finally ruined it by making the imperial hierarchy top-heavy much beyond the carrying capacity of the revenue base.

Following Max Weber's model of the patrimonial-bureaucratic empire, Stephen Blake has characterised the Mughal empire as one which closely corresponds to this ideal type. (Blake 1995) His main aim is to demonstrate that those who have described this empire as a modern centralised state have misunderstood its very nature. Patrimonialism means that the empire is treated as an extension of the imperial household. Interpreting Abu Fazl's *Ain-i-Akbari* along these lines, Blake supports his argument very well. However, one may also argue that the "discourse" of Abul Fazl and others was necessarily "patrimonial" while Akbar's practice went beyond that. In the measures described above he tried to substitute rules and regulations for individual decisions of the ruler. He was fairly successful in doing this. If one still wants to call his empire patrimonial-bureaucratic one must admit that it had rather modern features after all.

Unlike the Delhi sultanate which could not sustain dynasties for any length of time, the Great Mughals did once more establish a magnificent imperial dynasty. The secret of its success was the dynastic Darwinism which prevailed among the Mughals. Succession to the throne was not governed by primogeniture, any Mughal prince could try to succeed. This led to internecine struggles among the princes whenever a Great Mughal died, or even before he actually expired. The members of the imperial hierarchy took sides with the contending princes, but being on the wrong side did not affect their political fortunes. The victor might kill all his brothers, but he was keen to preserve the imperial hierarchy on which his rule would depend. In managing the hierarchy, the Great Mughal could rely on a system of checks and balances. He could freely transfer the imperial officers and he could also see to it that the commander of a strategically important fortress was a man equal or higher in rank than the respective provincial governor so as to establish a second line of direct imperial communication. The Mughal state was a highly sophisticated structure, and the Mughal dynastic charisma even survived when the Great Mughals were no longer very great.

Even at the height of its power the Mughal empire never controlled the whole subcontinent and in the seventeenth century rebellious regional forces such as the Marathas raised their head. But even they were deeply influenced by Mughal statecraft and copied much of it. The Mughals had adopted Persian as their administrative language and their successor regimes including the British retained the Persian revenue terminology. However, with all its great splendour and its strikingly modern administrative reforms, the Mughal empire more or less reproduced the platform-state of the Delhi sultanate. The alliance with the Rajputs and a policy of religious toleration enabled the Mughals to establish closer ties with their Hindu subjects. Their royal charisma which they consciously displayed helped to reinforce such ties. The rational design of the financial and military structure of their state enabled them to extend their rule more efficiently than the Sultans of Delhi. But the basic structure of their state was that of military feudalism superimposed on a peasant culture. The urban bias of the Mughal elite was very well expressed by the term "mofussil" (that which is separate) which encompassed everything which was distant from the centres of the empire.

The Commercialisation of Power in the Eighteenth Century

When Aurangzeb died in 1707 the Mughal empire practically ceased to exist though it lingered on as a shadow of its former glory for quite some time. It so happened that the two other great "gunpowder empires", that of the Ottomans and of the Safavids, also declined at about the same time. The Safavid dynasty of Persia was eliminated in 1722 and the Ottomans had to yield to the increasing pressure of the Habsburg empire and the rising power of the Russian Tsar. Indian historians have called this "the crisis of the eighteenth century" and since the latter part of that century saw the establishment of British colonial rule in India, the historians of India have generally depicted the eighteenth century as a dark age of weakness and decay which inevitably paved the way for India's subjection to foreign rule.

In economic terms the eighteenth century was actually a time of prosperity. Silver continued to pour into India, export production boomed. This was conducive to a commercialisation of power. Great traders emerged as financiers of various princes, granting credit to them while also acting as revenue farmers. (Bayly 1983) This was a pattern which was already well established in England where the commercialisation of power had flourished in the seventeenth century. (Braddick 1996) In fact, the East India Company was part and parcel of this development. It lent money to the king in return for the protection of its privileges. Thus it fitted in well with the commercialisation of power in India in the eighteenth century. But it had a decisive edge over its Indian contemporaries. The great Indian traders active in the commercialisation of power were individuals or at best families, the East India Company was a corporation with an administrative structure and a corporate memory. Its individual "covenanted servants" might be corrupt, in fact, they were expected to be corrupt, because they received meagre salaries and yet had to deposit an amount exceeding several annual salaries with the Company at the time of their appointment. They would forfeit this deposit if they acted against the interests of their employer, but they were otherwise expected to enrich themselves to their heart's content.

Due to the seize of its "investment", as the money transferred to India for buying goods was called, the East India Company soon became a major player in the Indian economy. In addition to being a great trading firm it was also a major naval power while Indian rulers concentrated on the land and neglected the sea. The naval power of the East India Company was of a peculiar kind. Since 1660 it had stopped building ships in its own dockyard and had started leasing ships, a very modern method, indeed. It could thus reserve its capital for the "investment" and shift the risk of financing ships to private shipowners who then tried to provide the best ships for hire as they were competing with each other. These ships were big, swift and armed with a large number of guns. Their captains were well paid and were therefore among the best navigators available anywhere. Since freight rates were high, these ships had to follow a strict timetable. But, of course, their armed presence in the Indian Ocean contributed a great deal to the political clout which the company had in India. The Peshwa Madhav Rao I saw this clearly when he said in 1767 that the British had put a ring around India.

At the time of this perceptive assessment of British power by a great Indian statesman, the Company had just acquired the Diwani of Bengal, bestowed upon them by a helpless Great Mughal who hoped to get a better deal from them than from the Nawab of Bengal whom they had vanquished. Actually this type of territorial control should have been assumed on behalf of the Crown rather than by the Company. But the British Prime Minister feared that the revenue of Bengal if it accrued to the ambitious King George III would diminish the influence of Parliament. This revenue should better flow into the private pockets of the directors of the Company, a decision in keeping with the idea of the commercialisation of power to which the

Parliament owed its great importance. This decision meant that the Company would remain as a buffer between the British and the Indian political system, it also implied that the Company would be gradually converted from a trading firm into an administrative agency governing India.

The Nature of the British Colonial State

The British captured India not as invaders but as interlopers. They hired Indian soldiers and paid them with the money of Indian taxpayers. This they could do by inserting their administrative machinery skilfully into the Indian political system. Like the mistletoe which flourishes on the branch of a tree from which it draws its sustenance, the British entrenched themselves in Bengal which was well suited for this purpose. The Nawabs of Bengal had made great progress in the commercialisation of power, they had eliminated the Mughal elite and relied on revenue farmers who provided them with a large revenue income in cash. Thus they had paved the way for the British who would have had no use for Bengal if they could not have siphoned off its revenue so very conveniently. As we have seen earlier, the Mughals had collected a very high land tax which dwarfed that of England. We also have to keep in mind that England had a population of about 5 million people in the eighteenth century whereas the erstwhile Mughal empire encompassed approximately 150 million people. Getting access to the revenues of India was thus like striking an enormous goldmine for the British.

The British faithfully copied the revenue systems of their predecessors. They also established law courts everywhere which helped them to secure the business of moneylenders who would help the peasants to meet the revenue demand. The peasants mortgaged their land to the moneylenders and were rarely able to redeem it. This ensured the moneylenders of a steady income from interest payments. (Rothermund 1978) The proliferation of law courts yielded additional revenue as the court fees far exceeded the cost of the judicial establishment. The

British colonial state was a parasite, but the British civil servants would not see it that way; they were usually convinced that they did their best for the people of India.

The Indian Civil Service which emerged from the "covenanted service" of the East India Company was an elite bureaucracy which in terms of its structure and its powers was well ahead of the bureaucracies of European states at that time. In many ways this service inherited the prestige and the functions of the Mughal mansabdars with the decisive difference that it was a "civil" service and not an elite of military officers entrusted with the tasks of civil administration. As a matter of fact, many of the early British civil servants in India were military officers before they joined the civil service, but they did so not in their military capacity, whereas the officers of the previous regimes were first and foremost military men throughout their career. This change of style from a military to a civil administration was also much more cost-effective. The British district officer with his small staff and comparatively austere habits was very different from the Mughal mansabdar with his cavalry garrison and his large number of retainers.

What has been said before about the rather barren platform-state established by the military regimes from the Delhi sultanate to the Mughals applied, of course, even more to the British colonial state. The British bureaucrats remained foreign with a vengeance, they derived their lifestyle from their home country to which they were going to return. The Mughal mansabdar would patronise artisans and dancers, musicians and poets. His British successor would do nothing of this sort, he would save all his money for buying a house at home. Urbanity dwindled in India under British rule, the process of cultural rustication which had begun under the earlier military regimes was completed by the British. The degree of urbanisation in the interior of the county receded. The only compensation for this was the growth of the port cities of Calcutta, Chennai (Madras) and Mumbai (Bombay). They became visible symbols of the colonial state. They also housed the first colleges and universities, the High Courts, the legislatures etc.

Undoubtedly the impact of the British colonial state on institution building was so strong that it practically prevented the consideration of any alternatives. The structure of educational institutions including their syllabus and curriculum, the statute books filled with innumerable laws, the constitutional framework, the civil service – all these remained deeply ingrained in the political culture. To varying degrees these institutions still shape the destinies of the states of South Asia even to this day. Nationalists had hardly any chance to change the course of colonial institution building. Attempts at establishing institutions of national education were bound to fail as only certificates recognised by the state served as passports for future careers. Ideas of framing a constitution different from that emerging from the tortuous process of colonial constitutional reforms were hardly ever discussed. In fact, the very process of constitutional reform rivetted the attention of the nationalists on the goal of undiluted Parlamentarism. The British could not grant it to their colonial subjects as it was incompatible with the maintenance of an irremovable executive. But the more it was denied to them, the more these subjects considered it to be the only aim worth striving for.

In their tortuous approximation of the parliamentary form of government the British constitution makers queered the pitch of India's political development. By introducing separate electorates for Muslims in 1909 and then granting "responsible government" in 1919 which – as the Secretary of State and the Viceroy jointly stated – was incompatible with separate electorates, they launched British India on the track which led to partition. (Rothermund 1965) The British, who often stressed that they considered the political unification of India as one of their greatest achievements, certainly did not intend to partition India. But finally they felt compelled to do it – a subject to which we shall return later on.

Nationalism and the State

Another development which proved to be a problem for the further course of events was the emergence of Indian nationalism along two very different lines. The model of the European nation state was received by educated Indians who attended the colleges and universities sponsored by the British. Great Britain was itself one of the most advanced nation states, and the Indians took it that the British ruled India due to this. In order to emancipate itself from British rule, India must also become a nation. The British taunted the Indians by pointing out that they were so divided in terms of castes, communities and language groups that they could never become a nation. There were two ways of responding to this challenge, the one was an evolutionary approach, the other a revolutionary one. India's liberal nationalists opted for the first one, they argued that India was not yet a nation but could become one by using the constitutional framework provided by the colonial state. The national revolutionaries rejected these British institutions and felt that they would only enslave India more and more. They believed that India had been a nation long ago and only needed to shake off the shackles of foreign rule in order to regain its earlier glory.

Those who believed in the national revolutionary creed turned to the past so as to find the roots of India's national solidarity. They created a solidarity traditionalism which left out all divisive elements and only highlighted those aspects of Indian history which fitted in with their vision of an Indian nation. The problem was that India had both a Hindu and a Muslim past. Nationalism spread first and foremost among the Hindus and they turned to the "golden age" of ancient India. The books of Western Indologists greatly helped them in their endeavour. The Muslims were left out of this reconstructed past, in fact, the more radical among the modern Indian traditionalists considered Muslim rule also as foreign rule and bracketed it with British rule. When nationalism finally affected the

Muslims, too, they turned to the Muslim past and blamed the British for having deprived them of their manifest destiny of ruling India. In this contest for different pasts the sober voice of the liberal nationalists who advocated secularism and looked to a common future of all Indians receded into the background until their message was revived by Indian socialists who otherwise had no use for the liberals.

The development of Indian nationalism was then deeply influenced by the emergence of Mahatma Gandhi as a charismatic leader. Gandhi was not a liberal and he was not interested in constitutions. His ethics centred on individual conduct. The right of resistance to an unjust state was more important to him than ideas devoted to the building of a national state. Some critics have called him an anarchist, but this is not true. When he had to reorganise the Indian National Congress so as to make it an efficient instrument of the freedom struggle, he carefully redrafted its statute and even thought that finally this statute could serve as a blueprint for a constitution of independent India. He shared with the national revolutionaries the idea that the British constitutional reforms imposed on India were instruments of slavery, but he was not at all interested in a quest for a useful past. He tried to awaken the Indian nation by appealing directly to the people. In this he was quite successful, but his enthusiasm could also lead him astray. This was particularly obvious in his relations with the Indian Muslims.

For the Muslims religion and the state are intimately related and since the Indian Muslims could not establish any relation with the British-Indian state they were attracted to Pan-Islamism. The Ottoman Kalif meant more to them than to his own subjects. When the British turned into enemies of the Kalif in the First World War, this converted many Indian Muslims into ardent nationalists. They were even more incensed when the victorious British deprived the Kalif of the control over the holy places of Islam. This gave rise to the Khilafat movement which Gandhi embraced rather uncritically. His rival M.A.

Jinnah, a liberal nationalist, knew about the ephemeral nature of this movement which appeared to him utterly reactionary. Jinnah was right, but Gandhi disregarded his warnings. He took the concern of the Khilafatists at face value and felt that their movement provided him with a golden opportunity to draw them into the mainstream of Indian politics. Initially this worked, but when in 1924 the Turks got rid of the Kalif, the Indian Muslims became political orphans and parted company with Indian nationalism. They were finally adopted by Jinnah who turned from a liberal nationalists into a communal leader who finally announced in 1940 that Hindus and Muslims are two nations – "by any definition of the term".

At this juncture the tortuous course of British-Indian constitutional reforms which had queered the pitch of India's future development and the demise of liberal nationalism as well as the rise of radical, agitational nationalism converged so as to lead to the tragedy of a partition which nobody had really wanted.

The Tragedy of Partition

The partition of India was tragic not only in terms of its immediate aftermath but also with regard to its long term effects which we witness today when two nuclear powers face each other in South Asia. Many studies have been devoted to the question of how a partition could have been averted and when the parting of the ways became inevitable. I do not wish to summarise these studies, but I may add my own judgement here: If the new Labour government immediately after coming to power in July 1945 had issued a clear declaration, announcing the date of India's independence and outlining the procedure of implementing this, there would have been no partition. The Labour Party was believed to be basically in favour of Indian independence. The problem of securing India's national debt which the Indian nationalists had threatened to abrogate had disappeared during the war from which Great Britain emerged as a debtor to India. Under these conditions one could have expected that the Labour Party would have a contingency plan concerning India which could be implemented on coming to power. But obviously there was no such plan, and even worse, there was no declaration until Lord Mountbatten was sent to India as the last Viceroy in 1947. Mountbatten refused to accept this assignment unless the government issued the declaration which was overdue. In the meantime precious time had been wasted and the British had permitted Jinnah to veto all constitutional proposals.

Jinnah had played a risky game, if the British had called his bluff he would have lost his control over the Muslim League. With every successful veto his political power increased. He probably wanted to use the demand for Pakistan as a bargaining counter so as to reach an agreement on a kind of confederation. The "moth-eaten Pakistan" as he himself called was not his aim. In fact, when Mountbatten compelled him to accept partition along the lines imposed by the British, Jinnah refused to say "yes". He merely nodded and Mountbatten accepted this tacit consent.

Mountbatten was a man of decisive action but not of much constitutional imagination. He did not even recognise the implications of a "Plan Balkan" which was returned to him from London with some "improvements" which meant the transfer of power to the provinces of British India rather than two dominions. In this way the wise men in London had wanted to avoid the odium of partition, leaving it to the provinces to arrive at whatever agreement they would prefer. Mountbatten showed this plan to Nehru and was surprised that Nehru was furious when he read it. Nehru immediately realised that "Plan Balkan" when implemented in this way would really mean the balkanisation of India as the provinces would be tempted to go it alone and forget about a central government. Under such conditions the princely states would also attain individual independence. After taking note of Nehru's objections, Mountbatten saw to it that the plan was suitably revised so as to enable the British to partition India as a final administrative act without any reference to the people concerned.

"Plan Balkan" did make the Congress leaders more amenable to the scheme of partition as it showed them an alternative which would be far worse. Finally even Gandhi gave up his resistance to this measure which he had called "the vivisection of India". The experience of the partition then made both successor states more self-consciously centralist. But although they both had the same constitution as enshrined in the "Indian Independence Act", their political style differed from the very beginning. In Pakistan Jinnah opted for the position of the Governor General and not for that of the Prime Minister like Nehru did in India. The constitution itself was flexible. It was deeply influenced by the viceregal heritage and could be worked in terms of a presidential system with the prime minister as a kind of assistant to the head of state. It also permitted the introduction of the conventions of British parliamentary government. In becoming Governor General Jinnah prevented the growth of parliamentary government in Pakistan while Nehru set an inspiring example for parliamentarism in India. However, both these forms of government, the presidential as well as the parliamentary one are highly centralist and they became even more so in India and Pakistan because of their mutual threat perceptions.

The Independent States of South Asia

In discussing the role of the state in South Asia we should not forget that there are two states which remained unaffected by the heritage of British India: Nepal and Sri Lanka. Of course, both these states were also deeply influenced by the British presence. Nepal remained an independent Hindu kingdom only because the British tolerated it as a convenient buffer state whose direct control would have been costly without adding any benefit to British rule. Ceylon, as Sri Lanka was called when it was a British crown colony, actually experienced a much more intensive colonial rule than most parts of British India. In the 19th century its population could be compared to that of one of the larger districts of British India and yet it had the full paraphernalia of a Governor in Council, legislature and High Court etc.

The Nepalese Hindu kingdom owed its emergence as a central state to the Gorkha ruler Prithvi Narayan Shah who captured Kathmandu in the late 18th century. His dynasty was soon superseded by the Ranas who like the Shoguns of Japan ruled the state and kept the king under virtual house arrest. The Ranas knew very well that they had to be in the good books of the British in order to maintain their power. When the British left India, the days of the Ranas were numbered. In 1951 King Tribhuvan fled to India and was reinstated in Nepal with Indian support. From then on the Shaha dynasty once more ruled Nepal. Tribhuvan knew very well that he could rely on Indian support only if he made concessions to the Nepal Congress whose leaders had been in exile in India when the Ranas ruled the country. The cohabitation of monarchy with democracy came to a sudden end when Tribhuvan's son Mahendra suspended the democratic government in 1961 and flirted with China after India had been defeated by the Chinese in the border war of 1962. Mahendra also showed a great deal of sympathy with "guided democracy" as practised by Ayub Khan in Pakistan. He replaced the Parliament with a National Panchayat, thus doing away with national parties who could challenge his autocratic rule. Mahendra's son Birendra who ascended the throne in 1972 at first continued his father's policy. Having studied at Harvard University he was supposed to be more open to modern ideas and he finally did manage the transition to democratic rule, but only after considerable internal strife.

By contrast Sri Lanka was firmly set on a democratic path even earlier than British India. Universal adult suffrage was introduced in 1931, but whereas one would have expected this to lead to political mass mobilisation it actually strenghtened the hold of an educated liberal oligarchy on the politics of the island. This was due to the peculiar political model which the British adopted for their constitutional reform of 1931. It was not Parliament but the London County Council which served as a model for the Ceylon legislature as well as its government. Thus Ceylon was governed like a municipality. Since there was no freedom movement, political life was quiet and unspectacular. Elite consensus was disrupted only several years after the grant of independence when Solomon Bandaranaike tried to reach out to the people who had only received education in Sinhalese (*swabhasha* educated) and could not aspire to the jobs which required a knowledge of English. His slogan "Sinhala only" offended the Ceylon Tamils. This marked the beginning of a deadly ethnic conflict which has not yet been solved. Bandaranaike was shot by a Buddhist monk who was dissatisfied with the slow pace of his political actions. Ever since then the beautiful island has proceeded on a course of increasing violence. The state was unable to cope with the bitterness of ethnic conflict.

In 1971 a new nation joined the circle of South Asian states: Bangladesh. The two wings of Pakistan had never lived happily together. West-Pakistan had treated East-Pakistan like a colony and had tried to suppress its Bengali language. As long as an artificial equilibrium could be maintained between the two wings by means of "guided democracy", West-Pakistan remained in control. But the first general elections upset this balance. Mujibur Rahman and his Awami League obtained a majority and should have formed the national government. The politicians of West-Pakistan could not tolerate this and secession became inevitable. In fact, the secession was mutual. Many felt that it had exploded Jinnah's "two nation"-theory. It had, indeed, shown that Islam was not a sufficient base for the creation of a two-winged state like Pakistan. The rise of Bangladesh meant that the Muslims of the subcontinent were now more or less evenly divided as the Muslim populations of India, Pakistan and Bangladesh were about the same size.

Unlike India which maintained democratic rule throughout and kept the military firmly under civilian control, Pakistan and Bangladesh experienced frequent military coups and long periods of military dictatorship. Interestingly enough, military coups in both these states followed the same pattern which is rather different from that observed in other states. Whereas elsewhere coups are usually staged by colonels who are in direct control of troops, the successful coups in Pakistan and Bangladesh were always headed by the commander-in-chief. The general concerned then became Chief Martial Law Administrator und turned into a President in due course. Right from the foundation of Pakistan the bureaucracy and the army had been the main pillars of the state and parties and politicians were at the most tolerated as a necessary evil. In recent years democracy has made some headway in both states but it is still in a precarious condition.

The stability of democratic rule in India owed much to the "Congress system" astutely managed by Nehru. With the prestige of the foremost organisation of the Indian freedom movement, the National Congress could continue to provide India with unchallenged political leadership for a long time. The majority election law which is otherwise supposed to produce a two-party system strengthened one-party rule in India, because the opposition was split into leftist and rightist parties and three-cornered contests always favoured the Congress as a centrist party. Nehru saw to it that it that it remained in the centre by veering slightly to the left and then to the right so as to steal the thunder of potential rivals. Nehru was also very keen to use the democratic national state as an instrument for supporting India as a nation in the making. In this respect his views were quite close to those of the liberal nationalists of an earlier time. He was deeply interested in India's past as his "Discovery of India" shows. But he did not sing the praise of an ancient Hindu India as the national revolutionaries had done. In fact, he was deeply concerned not only to bridge the gap between the two pasts, the Hindu past and the Muslim past, but also with making the Muslims of India feel at home in this country. His critics feel that in this he was bending over backwards as he surrendered to Muslim orthodoxy and did not dare to impose a uniform civil law on Hindus and Muslims alike.

Nehru's successors were less circumspect in maintaining the delicate balance of the "Congress system". They took it for granted and finally contributed to its decay. They also did not hesitate to play the "Hindu card" as the Hindus are after all the majority in India. In doing this they paved the way for a party which is openly wedded to Hindu nationalism, the Bharatiya Janata Party (BJP). This party aims at replacing the Congress as the centrist party, but in order to get into this position it has entered into all kinds of alliances with regional parties which have flourished in India in recent years. The Congress did not do this, because it would have compromised its centrist position by entering in such alliances. The BJP being clearly identified as a rightist party did not need to have any qualms in this respect, it could court allies of every sort. Thus it succeeded to form a coalition government in 1998. Actually both the BJP and Congress got 26 per cent of the national vote each, but the BJP captured more seats and could bank on its numerous allies.

Indian democracy is in a very precarious position at present, but the Indian state is still fairly stable and may continue to have the role which Nehru felt it should play - providing a framework for India as a nation in the making. In assessing the role of the state from this point of view we may turn to some thoughts expressed recently by P. V. Narasimha Rao who was Prime Minister of India from 1991 to 1996. Instead of writing memoirs, Narasimha Rao produced an autobiographical novel: "The Insider". This literary device helps him to look at the life of a politician from the detached point of view of the narrator. And it is in this capacity that he occasionally enunciates some words of political wisdom which transcend the story which he has to tell.

The State and the Hiatus between Desire and Capability

At one point he comments on the hiatus between desire and capability which generates a sense of discontent. This could refer to individual human beings as well as to whole societies. If human beings feel this sense of discontent they must try to strive for an equilibrium. He then asserts: "The same applied to the nation as a democratic entity. This was where man's most potent institution, the state, assumed crucial importance. If the state deployed its power to step up the hiatus further, the organism would break at some point. Sometimes it would break explosively; sometimes it would splinter into a web of hair-thin filaments like the windshield of a car at which a brick has been hurled, breaking into a maze of hair-thin cracks, noiselessly, yet making the shield permanently unstable und unsafe." After this warning he recommends: "The state, then, had to employ its power judiciously to counter the hiatus. To that end, it had to support the disempowered, and protect and assist the weak. It had to neutralize social imbalances, for whatever reason and in whatever manner these were manifest ..." This is a tall order. It amounts to the establishment of a welfare state. In South Asia this can only be a regulative idea, not a plan which can be implemented in the near future. In fact, the hiatus between the desire for establishing such a state and the capability of actually doing so is great.

If we think of the "nerves of state" which have been mentioned before we find that the extractive capacity of the present Indian state surpasses that of the Mughal state. About 40 per cent of the national product is nowadays claimed by the state, but this national product is small in per capita terms. In view of this the state must aim at increasing the national product and streamlining its own activities so as not to squander scarce resources. Another urgent task is that of giving more scope to federalism and strengthening local government. The British had introduced federalism in India although they themselves operated a highly centralised system of government at home. They did this in the course of the devolution of power so as to contrate essential functions at the centre while delegating less important functions to the provinces. The successor governments of the independent states of South Asia have maintained a centralist tradition. However, encouraging federalism should not be seen as a weakening of state power but rather as a constructive way of strengthening it. Narasimha Rao's metaphor of the broken windshield provides a warning for all politicians who put too much strain on a brittle structure. The state has a long tradition in South Asia and will certainly not wither away, but it needs to be reformed in keeping with the interests of the people. Therefore it is very important to raise the question to what extent the capabilities of the state do match the desires of its citizens.

References:

Bayly, Christoper (1983), *Rulers, Townsmen and Bazaars. North Indian Society in the Age of British Expansion, 1770-1870*, Cambridge

Blake, Stephen (1995), "The Patrimonial-Bureaucratic Empire of the Mughals",in: Hermann Kulke (ed.) (1995), *The State in India,1000-1700*, Delhi

Braddick, Michael (1996), *The Nerves of State. Taxation and the financing of the English state,1558-1714*, Manchester

Chattopadhyaya, Brajadulal (1995), "Political Processes and the Structure of Polity in Early Medieal India",in: Hermann Kulke, (ed.), *The State in India, 1000-1700*, Delhi

Chattopadhyay, Brajadulal (1997), "'Autonomous Spaces' and the Authority of the State: The Contradiction and its Resolution in Theory and Practice in Early India", in: Bernhard Kölver (ed.), (1997), *Recht, Staat und Verwaltung im klassischen Indien* , München

Erdosy, George (1995), "City States of North India and Pakistan at the Time of the Buddha", in: Fr.R. Allchin (ed.), *The Archaeology of Early Historic South Asia. The*

Emergence of Cities and States, Cambridge

Halbfass, Wilhelm (1988), *India and Europe. An Essay in Understanding*, Albany

Kuhrt, Amélie (1995), *The Ancient Near East, Vol. I & II*, London

Kulke, Hermann (1995), "The Early and the Imperial Kingdom: A Processual Model of Integrative State Formation in Early Medieval India," in: Hermann Kulke (ed.), (1995), *The State in India,1000-1700*, Delhi

Stein, Burton (1995), "The Segmentary State: Interim Reflections", in: Hermann Kulke (ed.), (1995), *The State in India, 1000-1700,* Delhi (OUP)

Narasimha Rao, P.V. (1998), *The Insider*, New Delhi

Rissman, Paul C. and Y.M.Chitalwala (1990), *Harappan Civilization and Oriyo Timbo*, New Delhi

Rothermund, Dietmar (1965), *Die politische Willensbildung in Indien, 1900-1960,* Wiesbaden

Rothermund, Dietmar (1978), *Government, Landlord and Peasant in India. Agrarian Relations under British Rule, 1865-1935,* Wiesbaden

Rothermund, Dietmar (1986), *The German Intellectual Quest for India*, New Delhi

Subbarayappa, B.V. (1996), *Indus Script. Its Nature and Structure,* Madras

Witzel, Michael (1997,"Early Sanskritization. Origins and Development of the Kuru State", in: Bernhard Kölver (ed.) (1997), *Recht, Staat und Verwaltung im klassischen Indien* , München

*Originally published in Imtiaz Ahmad, Partha Ghosh and Helmut Reifeld (eds.), *Pluralism and Equality: Values in Indian Society and Politics*. Copyright Konrad Adenauer Stiftung, 2000. All rights reserved. Reproduced with the permission of the copyright holder and the publishers, Sage Publications India Pvt. Ltd., New Delhi, India.

2

THE STATE AND THE MARKET IN INDIA, 1757-1995

When Robert Clive defeated the Nawab of Bengal at Plassey, he founded a territorial state of a new type in India. The significance of this event emerged only due to subsequent developments. The battle of Plassey was a minor skirmish when compared to other Indian battles of that time. Clive owed his victory more to treachery than to military superiority. He rewarded the traitor by making him the new Nawab of Bengal. This rich province was soon appropriated by the East India Company.

The British David defeated the Indian Goliath not at once, but step by step. The population of Great Britain amounted to about five per cent of that of the erstwhile Mughal empire. Looking back it appears to be unimaginable how such a small European country could conquer such a vast empire, the more so as the number of British posted in India was always very small. India was conquered by Indian mercenaries paid by Indian taxpayers.

Since India was now ruled by a company of traders, one should have thought that this would pave the way for its rapid development along the lines of free trade. But this company established a parasitical symbiosis with the Indian agrarian state. It enhanced the collection of land revenue, it eliminated Indian middlemen from the trade in cotton textiles and forced the weavers to sell their wares at the cheapest price. The company then transferred the surplus abroad which it had amassed in this way, whereas Indian rulers had spent their revenue income in India and thus recycled it within the country. The British drained the market of resources and liquidity. Thus the prosperity of eighteenth century India was turned into dismal poverty in the first half of the nineteenth century when deflation depressed prices.

This deflation was due to the reversal of the current of silver which had poured into India in earlier years due to the demand for Indian textiles, but was then siphoned off by the British once they gained more and more territory from which they could extract land revenue. The demand for Indian textiles also dwindled once British industrial products entered the market. Nevertheless, for quite some time many Indian weavers could still make both ends meet. With cheap food and cheap cotton they could produce textiles for the home market which could compete with industrial imports. But they could do so only by exploiting themselves and their families. (Specker 1984) The Bengal weavers, however, who had worked mostly for the export market suffered a severe setback. The report about "their bones bleaching in the plains of Bengal" which was later on quoted by Karl Marx was probably true.

Impoverished India did not provide an attractive market for British goods, but it did supply agricultural produce which could be sold at a profit by British entrepreneurs. Opium was produced by Indian peasants and monopolised by the East India Company which then sold it to private traders who smuggled it into China. Indigo was another product of Indian peasant agriculture which found a ready market abroad. Indian entrepreneurs were mostly excluded from this lucrative trade. When they managed to barge in, they would sooner or later be defeated. This is shown by the case of Dwarkanath Tagore, the grandfather of Rabindranath Tagore. He had bought up landed estates surrounding the indigo factories of the East India Company. When in 1833 the company was deprived of its last economic privileges by an act of Parliament, it had to sell those factories for a nominal amount to Tagore, because nobody else could hope to get access to them. He could then process indigo in those captive factories and make a handsome profit. When the price of indigo fell his firm as well as the Union Bank which he had founded went bankrupt whereas most of the British agency houses in Calcutta survived. (Kling 1976)

Investment in Railways and the Return of Silver to India

In Great Britain the railway age had ushered in the second stage of industrialisation after the earlier rise of the textile mills. Whereas such mills had mostly been financed by the respective entrepreneurs from accumulated savings and private loans, the railways required massive investment in terms of stocks and bonds. The British public got used to this, and when Great Britain was bustling with railways, the vision of the investors extended to the vast expanse of America and other countries overseas. India was also considered to be a target for such investment. The Governor General, Lord Dalhousie, who had earlier served on the railway board at home, designed a railway network for India in 1853 which encompassed 5000 miles. (Gadgil 1924) Now silver poured once again into India after nearly hundred years of deflation. Karl Marx predicted a rapid industrialisation of India at that time, because he thought that rails, engines and wagons would have to be manufactured in India. This then would have linkage effects and stimulate general industrial growth. He could not know at that time that the opening of the Suez Canal and the fall of freight rates for the shipment of goods by steamer would soon enable British industry to supply everything for the Indian railways. This was a boon for Great Britain, but not for India. Moreover, British investors received a guarantee of 5 per cent on their railway bonds which was high in this age of low interest rates. Being thus assured of their income, they could not care less for the profitability of the Indian railways which actually did not yield a profit until the turn of the century. In the meantime the Indian taxpayer had to foot the bill.

The silver which had returned to India due to the railway investment was soon joined by more of it as the silver price fell after 1876 and several European countries demonetised silver, depressing the price even further. In fact, if India had not absorbed a great deal of this silver, the price of this metal would have fallen even more rapidly. London was the centre of the world silver trade.

Keeping the Indian mints open to the free coinage of silver Rupees was therefore of great interest to the British silver traders. The Government of India did keep the mints open until 1893, but then it was forced to close them and to convert the Rupee into a token currency. The reason for this was that the revenue income of this government was in silver, but it had to remit the "Home Charges" in gold. When it could no longer make both ends meet, the closure of the mints was inevitable. As long as the silver flowed freely into India, it stimulated a slow and steady inflation and shielded the prices of Indian produce from the decline of the (gold) prices of produce in the world market.

In this period the extension of the railways also added to the rise and stabilisation of Indian agrarian prices. Whereas before 1885 there had often been both seasonal and regional price fluctuations, the national market established by the railway network eliminated these fluctuations to a large extent. But whereas the internal price (in silver) rose, the external one (in gold) fell and India actually exported wheat at the cheapest rate. Thus it helped to depress the wheat price in the world market while at the same time supporting the silver price due to its large scale absorption of this metal.

Due to the internal price rise of wheat and cotton, the advantage of the local weavers mentioned above disappeared and they could no longer face industrial competition. This also helped the nascent Indian textile industry. The first cotton mills had been established in the 1850s, but a rapid increase in the number of mills as well as of their output could only be registered in the last quarter of the nineteenth century. Of course, they could not expect any protection of the kind which Friedrich List had advocated for infant industries. On the contrary, when this industry could derive some small advantage from an import duty imposed for purely fiscal reasons, the British textile industry saw to it that this was accompanied by a "countervailing excise" on Indian textiles sold in the home market. But the Indian textile industry, almost exclusively owned by Indian entrepreneurs, survived and even competed with British industry by exporting yarn to East Asia.

The railway network also helped to distribute the products of Indian mills, but the structure of this network and the way in which freight rates were computed did not contribute to a harmonious development of the home market. The railway lines extended from the major ports to the regions in which agricultural produce was grown for export. Cross connections were few and far between. The freight rates were cheapest for long distance transports on a single line, transfers to other lines were more expensive. (Hurd 1983) This is how the differences of freight rates could have a great impact on the market. In general, one could state that the British aimed at linking India with the world market and that they paid attention to the Indian home market only to the extent that it contributed to this aim. Import substitution was, of course, undesirable in this context.

The Evolution of the Land Market and the Rise of Land Prices

Whereas British rule in India did little for the development of the Indian home market, it did contribute in a remarkable way to the extension of the land market and the steady rise of land prices. This rise in prices was not at all justified by increases of productivity in terms of yield. The growth of sharecropping even reduced the yield per acre as sharecroppers wish to maximise the returns to labour rather than to land. They opt for extensive rather than intensive agriculture. This raises the question why landowners rent out their land to such sharecroppers. They do so mostly when they are absentee landlords and earn their living elsewhere, treating the income from their land as a welcome addition to their income from other pursuits. And yet, inspite of declining yields land prices would rise, because social prestige was attached to the ownership of land and the growth of population ensured that land was a scarce commodity which could only appreciate in value.

The British land revenue administration guaranteed land titles although there was practically no proper record of rights. The revenue officers registered the land only for the purposes of revenue collection, they could not care less who owned the land as the land of revenue defaulters could be auctioned under the law of land sale. In fact, buying land at an auction was the most secure land title. But otherwise revenue receipts were also considered to be a presumptive proof of rightful possession. The innumerable judgements of the ubiquitous law courts also helped to secure titles to land. Many landowners had boxes full of such documents which were more valuable than mere revenue receipts. Court fees were high. They yielded an additional revenue to the state. Litigation was rampant and land titles were the most common object of such litigation.

Land prices also rose due to the fact that labour was cheap and plentiful. There was hardly any industry which competed for labour with agriculture. In 1913 the value of landed property at current prices was 40 billion Rupees whereas the total investment in Indian industry amounted to 300 mill. Rupees. (Goldsmith 1983) There was thus a vicious circle: investment in land competed with investment in industry and since industry remained of marginal importance, it did not attract much labour. Buying land, however, was a good proposition as long as one could get it cultivated at low wages.

The land market was directly connected with the credit market, because land was the chief collateral for getting credit. Mortgages and bonds were protected by British law which was designed so as to protect the creditor. This law was based on the presumption that debtor and creditor were contracting partners of equal status. This was, of course, not so in rural India where the debtor was usually a peasant who could not read or write and the creditor was a wily moneylender. Peasant indebtedness was mostly induced by the revenue demand. The moneylender would gladly pay the revenue on behalf of his debtor and get a mortgage which would keep the peasant permanently in debt. Very often the moneylender was also a grain dealer who pre-empted the harvest of his clients. Nominal interest rates were usually very high, whereas effective interest rates were geared to the actual conditions of the debtor. After all, the creditor was interested in keeping the debtor alive. The close supervision of credit by the moneylender was, of course, a costly affair and he could take on only a limited number of debtors, because he would not be able to control too many of them.

This type of control also enabled the creditor to tell the peasant what he should cultivate. Market signals thus travelled very fast to the remotest village. Although India was characterised by small-scale peasant agriculture, the whole country could be run like a plantation for the world market due to this network of credit and trade. British officers and Indian nationalists were fully aware of the sufferings of indebted peasants. The ideas of Raiffeisen, the German pioneer in the field of rural credit cooperatives, were well know in India. But the credit cooperatives established in India did not work properly. In most cases they were made use of by moneylenders who refinanced their operations in this way. The German village schoolmaster who was the linchpin of the Raiffeisen's system was missing in India. In Germany this schoolmaster was a government servant who was respected and trusted in his village for his learning as well as his integrity. He could act as an impartial and efficient registrar of the local credit cooperative.

The Emergence of a Dual Labour Market

While British law set the rules for the credit and land markets, British labour legislation had a crucial impact on the emergence of a dual labour market in India. This is evident even today. Ignorant observers have sometimes thought that the protection of factory labour was due to socialist ideas propagated in independent India, but the Indian Factory Acts were passed in 1881 and 1891 at the behest of British capitalists who wanted to prevent Indian industry from gaining undue advantage from cheap labour. Any plant employing more than hundred workers was subjected to these acts. (Gadgil 1924) There was thus a way of circumventing them by establishing small plants or hiring temporary labour. This dual labour market provided Indian industry with a great deal of flexibility. Indian industrialists always complained about the lack of skilled industrial labour in India. They deplored that most labourers remained peasants at heart and would disappear if they were needed at home. But in fact the industrialists benefited from fluctuations in the labour force and did not really care for permanently employed skilled labour. Textile mills could be operated by workers who were quickly trained on the job. Fluctuations in demand could be matched by the fluctuation of labour. Only a few positions in the mill had to be manned with skilled mechanics who knew how to keep it running. There was always a reserve army of labour at the gate of the mill.

In this context the "jobber" played a key role. He was both a foreman and a labour recruiter. He got paid both by the millowner and the workers whom he managed to get a job. The "jobber" was as important in the jute mills of Calcutta as in the cotton textile mills of Bombay. In Calcutta his position was even stronger. He could replace one worker with another at short notice. As there were several shifts, this created an additional possibility for cheating. Jobbers could keep "phantom workers" on their lists whose wages they could pocket with impunity. Sometimes 10 per cent of the labour forces were "phantoms" (Olbrecht 1993). The millowners tolerated these malpractices because they paid low wages and could rely on the jobbers who would keep the mill running, although at a low rate of productivity. Only the Great Depression forced the millowners to change their habits. They had to fire many workers in the 1930s. On the other hand the real wages of those employed rose due to the fall in agrarian prices. This made their jobs very attractive and they could be disciplined so as to raise productivity. The jobbers, however, lost much of their influence in the course of the depression.

World War and Great Depression

The British empire was at the zenith of its power on the eve of the First World War. The colonial state was so thoroughly entrenched that nothing seemed to be able to shake its foundations. Even the famines which had decimated the population of India at the end of the nineteenth century had not made a dent in the imperial armour. On the contrary, diminishing population growth caused by the famines had for the first time increased per capita income in India. The decade before the war was an era of complacency in British India. The integration of the Indian market into the world market had led to a rise in customs duties which now became the mainstay of government finance, replacing such earlier pillars of the budget as land revenue, the salt tax and the income from the opium monopoly which had been the mainstay of nineteenth century government finance.

But in the period from 1914 to 1945 British India was affected by global crises which destroyed the foundations of colonial rule. The sequence war-depression-war which was accompanied by shifts from inflation to deflation and back to inflation destabilised the colonial state and also affected the relations between the Indian home market and the world market. The First World War encouraged the Indian home market because it interrupted world trade and thus provided Indian industry with that kind of protection which had been denied to it by the colonial rulers in times of peace. Jamshed Tata, the Parsi industrialist, had founded a steel mill which started operating in 1907. This mill had required a large amount of investment which was completely derived from Indian sources. If peace had prevailed this mill would probably have been a failure, but government orders in the course of the war saved it. Other Indian industries benefited from the war in the same way. In the course of the war, the demand for investment goods increased very much, but because of the interruption of trade routes, this demand could not be satisfied. Therefore there was an unprecedented import boom in investment goods as soon as the war was over (Bagchi 1972). But the optimistic expectations of Indian industrialist were soon disappointed. They had to wait for the Second World War for a renewed upswing.

War time inflation led to a steep increase of agrarian prices. This was a boon for the landowning peasants, but not for labourers whose wages remained low. They were particularly affected by the sudden price rise after the bad harvest of 1918. The immediate postwar period was a time of social unrest. This also added to Gandhi's non-cooperation campaign. The impact of wartime inflation was more acute in India than elsewhere because India's currency still consisted for the most part of silver coins. The price of silver had risen steeply during the war and had remained fairly high in the immediate postwar period. This also supported the relatively high agrarian prices. During the Great Depression agrarian prices then declined by half and this dealt a severe blow to Indian agrarian markets from which they did not recover for a long time.

If Indian agriculture had been for the most part a subsistence agriculture, it would not have been affected by the depression. But as most peasants produced for the market under the combined pressure of revenue demand and debt service, the depression hit them hard. With their income halved they had to meet these charges practically at the same rate as before. Moreover, the moneylenders panicked, they not only refused to extend credit, they pressed for an immediate repayment of all debts. Therefore the peasants had to sell land or gold. The land-prices were supported in this way. They merely stagnated but did not fall in the years of the depression. The gold which the peasants sold in distress was exported. Thus India could register an export surplus even at the worst of times. A national government would have enacted an embargo on the export of gold and would have used it for reflating the economy. But the colonial government welcomed the stream of gold which enabled it to maintain the overvalued currency and thus prevent a flight from the Rupee. The British feared such a flight at the slightest indication of a devaluation, and they feared also that this would lead to a bankruptcy of the British government. The high exchange rate of the Rupee, however, amounted to an import bonus which benefited British traders exporting goods to India but restricted the chances of Indian exporters. The colonial government followed a severely deflationary policy and thus squeezed even more gold out of India. Politically this did not augur well for the colonial rulers. Peasants, traders, moneylenders and industrialists were all affected by this policy and flocked to the National Congress which rose to new heights under Mahatma Gandhi's leadership.

The Indian agrarian market was completely out of gear due to the impact of the depression. Wholesalers emptied their godowns and thus depressed prices even further. Forward trading which used to have a stabilising effect in the market was stopped. Regional and seasonal fluctuations which had practically ceased to exist after 1885 reasserted themselves with a vengeance. Prices remained depressed until the beginning of the Second World War. The basic economic rule that prices are determined by supply and demand did not work during the depression years. There was practically no change in production and consumption, in fact, the increase in population should have contributed to a rise in demand for grain. But the prices of all food grains remained at a low level. Rice was particularly affected although there was no overproduction of rice in the world market as that of wheat which had contributed to the onset of the depression. By 1933 rice was even cheaper than wheat in India – an altogether unprecedented phenomenon. In 1930 the rice price in India had still been rather high. In October the rice price fell in Japan where a good harvest and the deflationary policy of the government contributed to this decline. As Japan neither exported nor imported rice at that time, this should have remained a purely domestic affair. But the news travelled immediately to Liverpool and depressed the price of Indian rice there. By the time the winter rice harvest reached the markets of Calcutta and Rangoon in January 1931, the rice prices there were halved immediately and did not recover for quite some time. This was caused by credit signals travelling from the centres of the world market to the moneylender in the remotest Indian village (Rothermund 1992)

The Triumph of Protectionism

Under the impact of the depression the British gave up their attachment to the doctrine of free trade and opted for protectionism. With regard to India this was primarily due to the Japanese challenge. Japan reacted to the crisis by a radical devaluation of the Yen which reduced the prices of Japanese goods. It was a model case of aggressive "exchange dumping". The Indian textile industry was severely hit by Japanese competition, the more so as the British refused to devalue the Rupee. There was thus a loud clamour for protective tariffs in India. The British had already departed from their free trade policies after the First World War when they granted protective tariffs to the Indian steel industry which was hit by Belgian and German competition. But the new tariff regime for Indian steel included preferential rates for British steel. (Adarkar 1941) This amounted to an arrangement of market sharing in which the Indian industry had to acquiesce. It could serve as a blueprint for a similar arrangement of the cotton textile industry for protection against Japanese competition (Chatterji 1992). The colonial state and the market thus established an altogether new type of relationship. In 1931 protectionism was also extended to Indian wheat which faced the competition of Australian wheat. In normal times the British would have rejected such a measure outright as it violated imperial interests. But in this case political considerations prevailed, because the Panjab, the main wheat producing region, was also the home of most of the soldiers of the British-Indian army. It was essential to keep them loyal and satisfied.

After steel, textiles and wheat refined sugar also received the blessing of protectionism. India produced sugar cane in great quantities, but refined sugar had been imported from Java. Since no imperial interests were involved, the British encouraged the rather small Indian sugar industry with a protective tariff. Due to this measure, many sugar mills were established in the early 1930s. This was about the only major industrial investment in India in the years of the depression. By 1937 the Indian sugar industry had gone beyond import substitution and was eager to export sugar. But this would have hurt imperial interests, i.e. British planters in the Caribbean. Thus the world sugar agreement of 1937 classified India as a sugar importing country. This implied that it would not get a sugar export quota (Rothermund 1992). Market sharing was fine as far as the Indian home market was concerned, but it was ruled out for the world market.

The Rise of Interventionism in the Second World War

After India had come to appreciate the blessings of protectionism during the years of the depression, it experienced during the Second World War a powerful dose of state interventionism. It was thus not surprising that protectionism and interventionism concluded a happy marriage in independent India. At the beginning of the war, the colonial government was not at all prepared for such interventionism, in fact, it was rather complacent about the economic aspects of the war. The Viceroy, Lord Linlithgow, noted with relief that agrarian prices were rising and the peasants would thus have no further reason for being dissatisfied with the government. But as the war progressed, prices rose so steeply that the government had to try desperately to control the market. Once more the prices were not influenced by supply and demand, but rather by speculative trading. The war years were without exception years of good harvests. There was no food deficiency. But traders cornered the market and they were encouraged in this by the first inept attempts at state intervention. The government introduced price controls which did not help and only fostered the rise of a black market. Only at a later stage the government started buying grain and building up buffer stocks which permitted a direct intervention in the market (Knight 1954). But this could no longer prevent the terrible Bengal famine of 1943 during which millions of poor people died, because they could not afford buying rice which was available in plenty at high prices. In analysing this problem, Amartya Sen developed his idea of "entitlement". (Sen 1981)

Due to this terrible experience the government started issuing ration cards. By the end of the war about 100 mill. people had such ration cards. This was undoubtedly a major administrative achievement. At the beginning of the war the Government of India had no instruments of intervention of this kind. This was true of the market in food grains as well as of the procurement of war material (uniforms, boots, sandbags etc.) (Rothermund 1983) For procuring this material the respective Indian industries were not sequestered, but they had to produce goods ordered by the government at prices dictated by it. The respective authorities estimated the cost of production and added a 10 per cent profit margin. This was known as the "cost plus"- system, and in some sectors of Indian industry it still prevails. Even within this framework Indian industrialist enjoyed rich wartime profits which could be taxed only to some extent although special taxes were introduced for this purpose.

Wartime inflation was once more rampant, the more so as it could not be reigned in by a sufficient supply of consumer goods. Indian industry worked almost exclusively for the production of war materials and not for the home market. The Government of India printed money and subjected India to a system of forced saving. Whatever the British owed to India for wartime production was piled up as reserves in the Bank of England which India could not touch. The only benefit of this was that India turned into a creditor of Great Britain during the war. It thus earned its independence, because it is easier to grant independence to a creditor than to a debtor. After the war Great Britain was nearly broke and if India had wished to draw on the reserves in the Bank of England, this would have precipitated British bankruptcy. Accordingly India was made to sign a moratorium just before becoming independent.

India's Planned Economy: Interventionism and Protectionism

Independent India inherited protectionism from the depression and interventionism for the wartime economy. Without this heritage Nehru could not have established his planned economy as no instruments would have been available to him. Nehru's priority was the rapid expansion of Indian industry which had suffered under the impact of depression and war. The huge Indian home market made import substitution attractive whereas export-led growth was not considered to be a viable alternative. India's resources were limited and Nehru distrusted the forces of the market. He felt that competition was a luxury which only rich nations could afford whereas India had to save its scarce resources.

Nehru did not intend to nationalise the existing private industry, but he reserved the further expansion of basic industries for the public sector. The state should occupy the commanding heights of the economy. India's industrialists agreed with Nehru in this. They would much rather concentrate on producing consumer goods than engage in "capital deepening" required for the construction of heavy industry. The latter should be left to the taxpayer whereas private industry would invest in less risky enterprises which were more profitable in the short run. But the industrialists paid for this by accepting a regime of licences with which the state controlled the allocation of scarce resources. Of course, once an industrialist had got such a licence, he was hardly facing any risk at all and could be sure of selling everything he produced regardless of its quality. Indian industrialists had got used to operating under such constraints during the war. They had profited from it and would have felt much less comfortable in a fiercely competitive environment.

Foreign donors of development aid on which India depended once the reserves in the Bank of England had dwindled, were not at all interested in preaching liberalism to India at that time. India was a great customer in the field of industrial investment goods. Those who manufactured such goods were happy that development aid provided by the taxpayer saved them from giving credit to their customers from their own resources. Import substitution increased very rapidly in India, but India's share in world trade dwindled to insignificance. Initially there was hardly any complaint about this in India. India's subjection to the forces of the world market under British rule was not a happy memory and therefore almost everybody welcomed India's isolation from this market which was maintained for several decades.

Economic Development in India's Isolated Home Market

The Indian state succeeded in eliminating competition and subjecting production for the home market to its control. Since industrialisation had top priority, agrarian prices were deliberately kept at a low level in order to prevent a rise of industrial wages. The substantial increase of agricultural production during Nehru's time was almost exclusively due to the extension of cultivation. This meant that cultivation covered more and more of marginal soils which would have no yield if the monsoon failed. Under such conditions a catastrophe was predictable and it actually struck Indian in 1965/66 when two bad harvests in succession completely ruined the policy of low agrarian prices. This also affected the planning process and industrial investment which then stagnated for about a decade (Ahluwalia 1985). But this period of stagnation not only affected the public sector it also delayed the growth of the private sector. From 1955 to 1965 the share of the private sector in GNP had increased, but it decreased during the subsequent decade (Chandra 1981). The decline of public sector investment was not matched by a surge in private sector investment. This was typical for India's "mixed economy" with its lack of competition and its dependence on licences. In many respects the private sector enjoyed a free ride as long as the public sector expanded. When it stagnated, the private sector lapsed back, too. In the 1980s there was a new spurt of expansion of the public sector. The "free riders" jumped on the bandwagon, but this time they acquired such a momentum of their own that they continued to go ahead even when the public sector lost some speed. If one wishes to interpet this in a positive way, one could argue that Indian state capitalism has generated a development which is of a more sustainable kind than in other countries which have experienced similar regimes. A special feature of this Indian development is the rise of "regional capitalism" in several federal states of India (Baru 1994).

The "Green Revolution" has supported this kind of development. It led to a gradual upswing after 1970. Productivity increased, marginal soils were abandoned, irrigation was extended. Rising agrarian prices provided incentives to peasants to invest in technologies which are required for the "Green Revolution". Among the incentives for the peasants there was also the policy of the government which procured sometimes as much as 15 per cent of total grain production which were then released through a network of 400,000 "Fair Price Shops". This massive government intervention stabilised the agrarian market. It was, of course, a burden for the taxpayer, but the peasants who hardly paid any taxes took it for granted that this system must be maintained. As the peasants are also voters it is difficult for any party to challenge their privileges. Land revenue, the only tax paid by the peasants as peasants, has become only of symbolical significance ever since its enhancement had been affected by the Great Depression. It nowadays does not even cover the cost of its collection, but as revenue receipts are often the only proof of rightful possession, the peasants would resent its total abolition.

The National Congress initially profited from the fact that the peasants had been driven into its arms by the Great Depression. But in recent years being tied to the peasants is a liability rather than an asset in politics. The productivity of the peasants is limited, but their political clout is great. India is the second largest rice producer in the world, but it occupies only the 60th position with regard to yield per acre. Australia which occupies the first rank in this scale, produces about four times as much rice per acre as India does.

In breaking the political hold of the landowning peasants on India's political system, a political party might be tempted to side with the increasing number of landless labourers. They would certainly like to earn higher wages, but because their number is so great they are totally dependent on the peasants who hire them. Alternative industrial employment is so far not available to them.

The rise of agrarian production caused by the "Green Revolution" was followed by an upswing in industrial production only with a considerable timelag. This was also due to the oil crisis of the 1970s. There was an imported inflation in India because of this crisis. At the same time there was a curtailment of the supply of energy which affected industrial growth. In the period of low oil prices India had not intensified the exploration of its own resources of coal and oil. This was stepped up due to the crisis, but it took some time to yield impressive results. It was only in the course of the 1980s that a new industrial upsurge could be noted. (Ahluwalia 1991)

This upsurge was characterised by phenomena which had not been noted in earlier periods of Indian industrial growth. Productivity increased but employment did not rise to the same extent. This could be a statistical illusion, as only the "formal sector" is open to statistical scrutiny while the huge "informal sector" remains an "area of darkness". If a large amount of industrial production is farmed out to contractors in the informal sector, more productivity may be shown in the formal sector as "value added" accrues primarily to those who deliver the final product. The dual labour market which was earlier characterised by the difference between permanent and temporary labour has now transformed itself into a giant putting-out system. Factories in the formal sector are often only assembling the parts made in many small workshops. In this context one may speak of "diseconomies of scale" which cause a proliferation of this system. Factories in the formal sector suffer from the double impact of trade unions and taxation. Thus employment in the formal sector is only created to the extent that it is absolutely necessary for technological reasons.

According to recent calculations industrial growth is supposed to have amounted to 8 per cent per year in the period from 1980 to 1990. Agriculture has not been able to keep up with this rate of growth. Moreover, the growth of population always reduced the growth rate of the economy. There has been a modest growth of per capita income and life expectancy has risen, because the death rate has come down to a level approximating that of Europe. But the birth rate has not yet adjusted to the death rate. The surplus population is for the most part absorbed by the rural sector. It would drown the cities without this absorptive capacity of the countryside.

The bottleneck which is thus very clearly visible can only be overcome by a change of the market and the generation of productive employment. This can only be hoped for in the context of a new integration of the Indian economy in the world market – not the one which India had experienced under colonial rule, but one which is determined by India itself. Unfortunately the Indian government had taken the first steps in this direction by liberalising foreign trade rather than beginning with an internal liberalisation.

Liberalisation of Foreign Trade versus Internal Liberalisation

In the 1980s Indira Gandhi and Rajiv Gandhi embarked on a policy of liberalisation which took the line of least resistance. Prohibitive protective tariffs and outright import restrictions were removed and reduced tariffs applied to a wide variety of goods. This blessed the state with an enormous income from customs duties which are exclusively reserved for the central government. This was reflected in a rise of the share of the state in GNP and permitted the unreformed continuation of public enterprise which even increased employment during this period. Politically this was opportune in the short run, but it created, of course, further liabilities which soon showed up as impediments to liberalisation.

It is generally expected that after the initial liberalisation of foreign trade, imports will increase before exports surpass them. But in India export growth was rather limited and this led inevitably to a balance of payments crisis. Moreover, Indians abroad (NRI=Non Resident Indians) had parked their savings in India attracted by high interest rates and free convertibility. Once they became afraid of a balance of payments crisis they would actually precipitate it by withdrawing their funds. The crisis could be overcome only by a massive intervention of the International Monetary Fund with the support of the World Bank. In the summer of 1991 a new government under Prime Minister P.V. Narasimha Rao and Finance Minister Dr. Manmohan Singh did the needful, i.e. devalue the currency and reduce the budget deficit. Dr. Singh who had served a term with the World Bank did not need to be told what was expected of him. The measures adopted by the government also restored the confidence of the NRIs whose funds flowed back to India. Foreign investors were also attracted by the new policy. For a time it seemed that the relations between the state and the market had really been fully reformed.

But the heritage of the past could not be overcome that easily. Bureaucrats trained in decades of interventionism cannot suddenly adopt a new attitude. Public sector industries with their surplus labour which could not be easily dismissed constituted insurmountable obstacles to privatisation. Peasants who had got used to subsidies could not be told to forget about them unless one dared to face their wrath at the next elections. A further liberalisation of foreign trade would upset industrialists who were not yet ready to face the competition of the world market. Many of them had good reasons to fear that their industries would be wiped out if they were fully exposed to this competition. Thus the Indian state and the market will take quite some time to reform their relationship in the interest of economic growth and the eradication of mass poverty.

References:

Adarkar, B.P. (1941), *The Indian Fiscal Policy*. Allahabad

Ahluwalia, Isher Judge (1985), *Industrial Growth in India. Stagnation Since the Mid-Sixties*. Delhi

Ahluwalia, Isher Judge (1991), *Productivity and Growth in Indian Manufacturing,* Delhi

Aiolfi, Sergio (1987), *Calicos und gedrucktes Zeug. Die Entwicklung der englischen Textilveredelung und der Tuchhandel der East India Company, 1650-1750.* Stuttgart

Ambirajan, S. (1978), *Political Economy and British Policy in India,* Cambridge

Bagchi. Amiya K. (1972), *Private Investment in India, 1900-1939*. Cambridge

Baru, Sanjaya (1994), "Continuity and Change in Indian Industrial Policy", in: T.V. Satyamurthy (ed.), *Industry and Agriculture in India Since Independence*, Delhi

Bayly, Christopher (1983), *Rulers, Townsmen and Bazaars. North Indian Society in the Age of British Expansion, 1770- 1870*, Cambridge

Chandavarkar, Rajnarayan (1994), *The Origins of Industrial Capitalism in India. Business Strategies and the Working Classes in Bombay, 1900-1940*, Cambridge

Chandra, N.K. (1981),"Monopoly Capital, Private Corporate Sector and the Indian Economy: A Study in Relative Growth,1931-1976", in: Amiya K. Bagchi & Nirmala Banerjee (eds.), Change and Choice in Indian Industry, Calcutta

Chatterji, Basudev (1992), *Trade, Tariffs and Empire. Lancashire and British Policy in India, 1919-1939,* Delhi

Gadgil, D.R. (1924),*The Industrial Evolution of India in Recent Times,* Madras

Goldsmith, Raymond W. (1983), *The Financial Development of India, 1860-1977,* New Haven

Hurd, John (1983), "Railways", in: Dharma Kumar (ed.), *The Cambridge Economic History of India, Vol. 2,* Cambridge

Kling, Blair (1976), *Partner in Empire. Dwarkanath Tagore and the Age of Enterprise in Eastern India*, Berkeley

Knight, Henry (1954), *Food Administration in India, 1939-1947,* Stanford

Morris, Morris D. (1983), "The Growth of Large-Scale Industry", in: Dharma Kumar (ed.), *The Cambridge Economic History of India, Vol. 2,* Cambridge

Olbrecht, Urs (1993), *Der Alltag der bengalischen Jutearbeiter in der spätkolonialen Ära.* unpublished thesis (Lizentiat), Dept. of History, University of Zurich

Rothermund, Dietmar (1970), "India's Silver Currency. An Aspect of the Monetary Policy of British Imperialism", in: *Indian Social and Economic History Review 7*

Rothermund, Dietmar (1978), *Government, Landlord and Peasant in India. Agrarian Relations under British Rule, 1865-1935,* Wiesbaden

Rothermund, Dietmar (1983) "Die Anfänge der indischen Wirtschaftsplanung im Zweiten Weltkrieg", in: Peter Halblützel et al. (eds.), *Dritte Welt: Historische Prägung und Politische Herausforderung. Festschrift für Rudolf von Albertini,*, Wiesbaden

Rothermund, Dietmar (1992), *India in the Great Depression, 1929-1939*. New Delhi

Rothermund, Dietmar (ed.) (1996), *Liberalising India. Progress and Problems,* New Delhi

Sen, Amartya (1981), *Poverty and Famines: An Essay on Entitlement and Deprivation*, Oxford

Specker, Konrad (1984), *Weber im Wettbewerb. Das Schicksal des südindischen Textilhandwerks im 19. Jahrhundert*, Wiesbaden

Subrahmanyam, Sanjay (1990), *The Political Economy of Commerce: South India,1500-1650*, Cambridge

3

TOWN AND COUNTRY IN INDIA

"Town" means a place which is separated by a fence from the surrounding countryside. The ancient Indian term *durga* which refers to a fortified town literally means "difficult to enter". The Arthashastra lists *durga* as one of the necessary elements of sovereignty. It is the focus of dominance over the countryside. Its walls set it apart from the rural environment. (Laping 1982) This sense of separation was inverted in later periods of Indian history when Muslim rulers governed the country from their splendid capitals and referred to all places which were at some distance from this urban centre as *mofussil* (that which is separated). Even now this term has a negative connotation, it implies the isolation and the lack of cultural amenities which the urban officer would experience when he has to go out to such places.

Town and country were thus perceived as mutually exclusive spheres of life, but they also needed each other. Peasant society is incomplete without an urban focus, and the town could not survive without the surplus generated by its rural environment. There must be a give and take between town and country, unless the appropriation of the rural surplus is based on pure coercion. Whereas it is quite obvious what the town expects from the peasant, it is much more difficult to explain what it gives to him. There was a blend of religious, cultural and commercial ties which connected the countryside with the town. Pilgrimage and purchase would provide mixed motives for the peasant's visit of the town. Most towns were built around crossroads (*chowk*) which manifested the meeting and parting of ways. A construction of symbolic space was superimposed on this physical reality. (Kulke 1982) Temple and palace were located so as to represent this symbolic space visually; the peasant was impressed by such symbols of order referring to the world he lived in and the one beyond inspiring his religious imagination.

Crossroads attract market places and the urban control over rural surplus was often achieved by taxing rural commodities, which were bought and sold in the town. Even today huge Indian cities, like Bombay, derive the largest amount of their revenue from octroi, a tax levied on all goods brought into the city. This antediluvian method of taxation yields good returns at little cost to the municipality, because the humble collectors of this tax are able to improve their meagre legitimate income by petty exactions when using their discretion in the evaluation of goods. Similarly, early Indian rulers often depended more on the taxation of trade than on land revenue. Wherever intensive cultivation increased and the administrative machinery for the collection of land revenue could be put to work, this tax soon became the mainstay of royal power and of urban control over rural surplus. As long as the revenue demand was light, not much coercion was required for its collection. But, in later periods of Indian history increasing expenditure on cavalry warfare led to a high revenue demand, at the same time the man on horseback proved to be an effective revenue collector. New towns emerged which were primarily cavalry garrisons, but also served as commercial and administrative centres. Their relationship with the surrounding countryside was different from that of towns in earlier periods. They encroached forcefully on the autonomy of village institutions and made the local cavalry commander the linchpin of state authority in the urban and in the rural sphere. The changes in the methods of warfare and in military organisation thus had a profound impact on the relation between town and country in India. It is this impact which deserves to be explored in greater detail.

The Military Impact on the Relationship between Town and Countryside

Indian culture has been mostly articulated by priests and poets, and if Indian warriors were literate at all, they preferred to write poetry rather than reports on warfare.

For this reason the world of the warrior has remained mute in India with the notable exception of the *Mahabharata*, which gives a poetic account of warriors and their deeds. The incessant warfare in later periods of Indian history was so much taken for granted that nobody cared to write about it. The visual arts are different in this respect, they provide occasional glimpses of battle scenes. On the friezes of Indian temples, the innumerable dancers and musicians are sometimes joined by marching armies which are thus portrayed as features of everyday life rather than as extraordinary phenomena. In fact, much more of the rural surplus was invested in warfare in India than in most other countries. Accordingly, the military played a decisive role in shaping the pattern of urban settlements and regulating their relations with their rural hinterland.

When Max Weber tried to account for the role of the towns in his grand scheme of social analysis, he saw in their internal organisation the roots of non-legitimate rule and emphasized the revolutionary usurpation by which the citizens of towns wrested rights and privileges from superior legitimate authorities. Weber stated that they could do this in Europe because of a certain homogeneity and solidarity of the citizenry which, due to the rigid caste system, could never be achieved in India. (Weber 1964) Like so many Western social scientists, Weber was fascinated by that strange system of social order and tended to attribute too much to it. He also had hardly any idea of the internal organisation of Indian towns whose local government had a great deal of autonomy in some periods of history. This internal aspect of urban organisation is reflected by the term *nagara* (town, city). It has a connotation of urbanity, and it also refers to the commercial functions of the town and their autonomous regulation in the interest of everybody concerned. It is no accident that by a subtle shift *nagara* became *negara* (state) in the Malayan languages of Southeast Asia. The Indian model of political organisation which was transferred overseas manifested itself in its urban rather than in its rural context. The nagara-negara-model signifies legitimate rule and not Weber's non-legitimate rule based on revolutionary usurpation. It presupposes a harmonious symbiosis of kingship and urban organisation. Even in India, *nagara* could become synonymous with the respective state as in Vijayanagara, the name of a great capital, but also of a vast empire in South India. It is an irony of fate that this empire was dominated by an elaborate military organisation which did not at all correspond to the ideal model of *nagara* as outlined above. Military power tilted the balance in favour of the warrior king with his garrisons and armies against the harmonious symbiosis of king, market and temple found in the ideal *nagara*.

The Cavalry State and its Urban Organisation

The backbone of military organisation which determined the relation between town and country in India in the late middle ages was the maintenance of large cavalry contingents. Good war-horses were invariably imported as they could not be bred in India. The Indian countryside thus could not provide the towns of the warriors with horses, but the peasants had to foot the bill for this extravagant military investment. In the Delhi Sultanate of the 14th century a good war-horse fetched a price which was about thirty times that of a milch-cow. (Digby 1971) Thus when the sultan sent 100,000 horses to the battlefield this was equivalent to three million cows. According to contemporary reports the sultan's cavalry was often much larger than that, and the price of the horses was not the only burden which the taxpayers had to bear. For each horse there would be a skilled warrior and an experienced groom and other supporting staff, these people were mostly slaves whose prices were lower than those of war-horses, but they also had to be maintained. For Hindu rulers of the South who depended entirely on the import of horses by sea, the prices of good horses would tend to be higher. They had to pay for the losses at sea in order to keep the horse traders in business who usually had very good contacts with the royal court. The Persians, and later on the Portuguese, derived much profit from this trade.

The enormous cavalry contingents needed garrisons outside the capital and revenue was assigned to their commanders for the support of their horses and troops. This gave rise to a new type of urbanisation based on the forcible appropriation of rural surplus. If the inhabitants of such garrison towns were Muslims and the surrounding countryside remained the abode of a Hindu peasantry as in most parts of Northern India, the cultural ties between town and country became very tenuous. The town could no longer serve as the visual representation of a symbolic space which would attract the spiritual imagination of the peasant. The peasant would still visit the market in town and perhaps he would gaze at the warriors and their horses and admire the residence of the local commander, but all this was alien and awe-inspiring to him. The cultural synthesis embodied by such towns which also attracted urban Hindus remained permanently detached from the countryside. This was less so in the Hindu realms of South India where the rulers and the ruled still shared a common background, but even there the new military organisation created a rift between town and countryside. The commander and his troops were usually strangers from some other part of the country. They were mostly Indians, of course, and not immigrants from Central and Western Asia as the Muslim warriors in Northern India. But for the settled peasants even a man who came from another part of India and was only temporarily posted in the respective town would remain a stranger. The rulers knew this and used it to their advantage, because commanders of powerful cavalry contingents should never be permitted to grow local roots as this would enable them to challenge the ruler.

The military rulers also saw to it that the peasants could never dream of armed resistance. As long as the war-horse was the linchpin of their power, they were safe, because the peasants did not have the means to acquire such horses. But once they introduced firearms they could no longer be sure of such a monopoly. War-horses could not be bred in Indian villages, but primitive muskets could very well be manufactured by skilful village smiths. The countryside was stricking back and the towns lost control over it.

Town and Country under British Rule

Indian rulers had, with very few exceptions, always neglected the vast maritime periphery of India. Asian maritime trade was for the most part free and unobstructed by major sea powers. Therefore Indian rulers did not need to have navies in order to keep the channels of trade open. The Chola naval expedition against Srivijaya thus remained an isolated episode in Indian history. An invasion of India from the sea was inconceivable, as the monsoon was bound to interrupt the supply lines every year. Even a large expeditionary force would find itself literally stranded. The man on horseback could therefore afford to disregard the Europeans who approached India from the sea.

The British were prudent enough not to invade India by landing their troops which would have perished. They built up commercial bridgeheads over a long period of time and trained Indian mercenaries in modern infantry warfare. Initially, there was no plan behind this, the British were actually forced by the French to join this game of recruiting and training a native infantry. But once they had this infantry it proved to be an enormous asset. Neither armed peasants nor cavalry could stand up to disciplined infantry troops which would shoot volley after volley with the remorseless precision of a machine. There was another element of warfare in which the British surpassed the Indians: military finance. With very few exceptions, all great Indian warriors were hopelessly inept in this field: Even a victorious Indian army would quickly disintegrate if the paymaster was short of funds. Wars which were waged by a commercial company were well calculated risks. The British were cautious warriors and reliable paymasters. When they had conquered India by these methods, they did away with the expensive military organisation of their predecessors. Because their garrisons and their administrative functions no longer existed, many towns which had dotted the countryside dwindled to insignificance. Great numbers of people were literally rusticated and as the imperial capital of the British was abroad, the whole of India was *mofussilised*. Rather than the threat of brute force, bureaucratic efficiency was the mainstay of British rule.

The British claimed India's rural surplus to a larger extent than their indigenous predecessors, but it was no longer redistributed in the country by means of wasteful military expenditure and conspicuous urban consumption. The surplus was mostly transferred abroad. The office of the British district officer, who was appropriately called "Collector", was much more austere than that of the local cavalry commander under previous regimes. The transition from feudal splendour to a bourgeois lifestyle was also obvious in the residential quarters constructed for the new authorities. The "bungalow" in the "civil lines" rather than a palace in town was the abode of the British district officer. These new architectural features spread all over India and showed a striking uniformity. (Pieper 1992) The colonial settlements of government officers were neither truly urban nor actually rural, they were always constructed at a distance from the native town to which they were attached and projected a pattern of open spaces and gardens like the environment of English country houses. But they were also not part of the Indian countryside, and thus kept aloof from both town and country in a very peculiar way. When the British at the very end of their rule over India decided to build an imperial capital in New Delhi, they reproduced this pattern in monumental dimensions and created a gigantic "civil lines" with only a few large representative buildings thrown in for good measure. In Bombay and Calcutta, however, which grew over the centuries in a haphazard way, they reproduced the English urban style. But these cities were literally marginal to India and served as bridgeheads of maritime trade rather than as centres related to the Indian countryside.

The Urban Enclave and the Rural Hinterland

Under the impact of British rule, the relation between town and country in India was transformed into the relation between enclave and hinterland. Even the earliest British settlements in India, the factories of the East India Company, were typical enclaves whose relations with their hinterland were purely commercial. What they had to offer was a steady stream of precious metals which facilitated the monetisation of the land revenue demand and was thus very welcome to Indian rulers. After the British had made substantial territorial acquisitions in India and the industrial revolution had changed the nature of the English economy, some of the earlier bridgeheads grew to amazing proportions. The precious metals were now flowing out of India and industrial goods poured through these bridgeheads into the rural hinterland. With the decline of indigenous industries the rustication of India progressed very rapidly and the whole country was turned into a vast "hinterland". The life of the busy maritime enclaves was determined more by the development of the world market than by the hinterland.

In Calcutta, the greatest bridgehead of all, there was a peculiar relation between town and country. Many of the large landholders (*zamindars*) built veritable city palaces and indulged in conspicuous consumption. During the period when their fortunes were not yet dissipated they cultivated an urbane Bengali atmosphere open to all kinds of intellectual pursuits and literary experiments. This was a leisure class with a vengeance, it was hemmed in by the urban enclave which sustained it. Its ideas barely made an impact on the hinterland. The "country cousin" who lived on the family estate was often looked upon with disdain, but he was given some importance as long as he saw to it that rental income would steadily flow from the estate to the city palace. Litigation became a favourite pastime of this leisure class, and its more ambitious members became lawyers themselves as this was a prestigious profession. The Calcutta High Court was something like a secular temple for this new elite. The University of Calcutta had a similar stature, and the acquisition of academic degrees became the hallmark of elite status. When educated unemployment became a problem in Calcutta, the frustration of young people who aspired to this elite status was particularly severe. The rise of terrorism amongst them was a reaction to this frustration. They were bottled up in the colonial urban enclave and the cult of the bomb meant salvation to them.

The gigantic enclave Calcutta also spawned sub-enclaves which were related to the export-oriented industry of the colonial metropolis. There were tea plantations at the foot of the Himalayas and the coalfield enclave in the upper Damodar valley on the border between Bengal and Bihar. These enclaves were controlled by British managing agencies who owned plantations in the hills, collieries in the Asansol and Jharia fields, and jute mills in Calcutta. With the growth of the railways, the outreach of the major enclaves increased and a new type of small enclaves mushroomed all over India: the railway junctions. Occasionally such a junction would be located close to a *mofussil* district town, but more often it would spring up in the middle of nowhere and its functions would be restricted to the maintenance of the railway connections. The "civil lines" were reproduced here in a more modest way as "railway lines" where the railway staff resided. The urban centres which profited from the extension of the railways were ports like Bombay, Calcutta, and Karachi, but not the up-country towns. There were only few instances were such *mofussil* towns benefited to a large extent from the railway connection. Solapur in Maharashtra is a case in point. The railway reached Solapur in 1860 and for some decades it remained the railway terminal for the surrounding cotton country. In due course it became an important textile centre with several mills. Many skilled weavers from Andhra migrated to Solapur and contributed to its importance as a textile town. But the rise of an Indian up-country town in the colonial period was an exception which proves the rule that, in general, urban growth was restricted to the major ports.

Urbanisation proceeded very slowly in British India and it could be said that under colonial rule India was more rural than ever before. It was dominated by a kind of rural life which lacked an urban focus as a creative counterpart. Colonial ports, enclaves, "civil lines", and railway junctions simply could not play the role which towns had played in earlier periods of Indian history. The English-speaking urban intelligentsia of India was therefore much more isolated from the people in the countryside than the urban elite of earlier times. This is why the Indian freedom movement remained for a long time restricted to the urban intelligentsia and had no impact on the countryside. It was only due to Gandhi's endeavour to reach the rural people that the freedom movement slowly gained a foothold outside the restricted urban sphere. The Great Depression then gave added importance to this connection, because it hit the Indian peasants very severely, while it benefited the urban classes whose standard of living increased due to low food prices. The dichotomy between town and country was accentuated by the depression. If Gandhi had not prepared the National Congress for a rural role, it could have missed the boat and remained entrapped in its urban enclave existence. The British colonial rulers were actually convinced even at the time of the depression that the National Congress represented only an urban movement and could not affect the countryside. They were therefore greatly surprised when the substantial peasants, whom they had enfranchised so as to fortify the social base of their rule, voted for the National Congress. (Rothermund 1992) This represented an entirely new political contract between town and country in India and was of great consequence for the development of independent India.

Town and Country in Independent India

The National Congress had the mandate of the substantial peasantry of India which provided a great deal of stability to the political system after India had achieved independence from British rule. But the colonial heritage in all its various aspects still lingered on. The relation between town and country as it had been determined by the British could not be changed very easily. One of the features inherited from the past was the predominance of the trend towards metropolisation, i.e. the growth of the four major cities. The pace of this growth was much faster than urbanisation in general. Very few Indian cities could rival the four major cities. Bangalore in the South was one of the few exceptions. It had been founded by Kempe Gowda, a military commander of the Vijayanagar empire, and was thus one of the typical examples of the military urbanisation mentioned above. Later, it had prospered as the capital of the Maharajas of Mysore, and after independence its "rust proof" climate had attracted several branches of advanced technology (aircraft, machine tools, etc.). Nevertheless, due to its earlier role as the capital of a princely state, it had retained a more intimate relationship with the surrounding countryside than the steel cities of Eastern India. These cities Bhilai, Bokaro, and Rourkela remained isolated industrial enclaves with hardly any contact with their backward rural hinterland. This was also true of the faceless urban agglomeration in the coalfield around Jharia and Asansol, which has been mentioned earlier. This enormous enclave had hardly any positive relation with its immediate hinterland, at the most it gave some marginal employment to the poor people in the countryside, who worked in the open cast mines on the fringe of the coalfield. Most of the people working in the coalfield came from other parts of India and the food supply for these people arrived by truck or railway, and it was not produced in the immediate hinterland. The coalfield had begun as an enclave in the late 19th century and it had retained this character ever since. (Rothermund 1978 & 1980)

The persistence of enclave urbanisation is a typical phenomenon of Eastern India which has a high density of rural population, but only very few important towns. Western and Southern India are quite different in this respect. They have a higher degree of urbanisation and a more evenly structured hierarchy of cities, major towns and smaller towns. Leaving aside the two old port cities, Bombay and Madras, there is a string of cities with one million or more inhabitants from Ahmedabad in the Northwest via Pune, Hyderabad, and Bangalore to Madurai in the Southeast. They are followed by the next tier of large towns, such as Vadodara (Baroda), Surat, Solapur, Mysore, Coimbatore, Salem, Tiruchirapalli, and Trivandrum, which each have half a million or more inhabitants. But even in these more urbanized parts of India, there are millions of rural people who would migrate to towns and cities if they could get work there. In earlier periods of Indian history, it was only the control of rural surplus which was relevant for the town. In recent decades, towns were also supposed to absorb surplus labour which can no longer be gainfully employed in the countryside. Population growth has increased the problem of disguised rural unemployment, whose dead weight depresses agricultural development. If this unemployment would throw off its disguise and all surplus labour would rush to the towns and cities, they would collapse. Those who have tried their luck in the city and failed carry this message back to the countryside. This is the "push-back" factor which outweighs the "pull" factor of rural-urban migration. (Bose 1971) In this way a new dimension has been added to the relation between town and country in India.

The inability of the towns to absorb surplus labour from the countryside delays the demographic transition in India which has been witnessed in European industrial countries as well as in Japan. In those countries a reduction of the birth rate followed the reduction of the death rate with a time lag of one generation. This rapid transition was obviously due to a change from a rural to an urban life style for all those who participated in one way or the other in industrial production. If people who wish to adopt an urban life style in order to make a living are "pushed back", they are not going to contribute to the demographic transition. On the other hand, the control of public health in the countryside by means of modern urban medicine has reduced the number of epidemics, and thus lowered the death rate, and nobody could wish to raise it again. Town and country are thus caught on the horns of a dilemma. The town has to keep the country at arm's length in order not to be swamped by unwanted surplus labour, but in doing this, it increases the pressure which is building up in the countryside. In India this dilemma has to be faced at close quarters, but, in fact, it is a global one: the rich, industrialized North is in the same position vis-à-vis the poor, rural South. The modern mass media in India and elsewhere constantly increase the awareness of urban life style among the rural poor. They receive inviting messages but must stay where they are, and whereas actual experience may result in a "push back", the messages which radiate from the town to the countryside still have a seductive pull-effect.

References:

Bose, Ashish (1971), *India's Urbanization, 1901-2001,* New Delhi

Digby, Simon (1971), *War-horse and Elephant in the Delhi Sultanate.* Oxford

Kulke, Hermann (1982), "Legitimation and Town-Planning in the Feudatory States of Orissa" and Gutschow, Niels, "Patan: Symbolik einer newarischen Stadt in Nepal", in: H. Kulke et al. (eds.), *Städte in Indien,* Wiesbaden

Laping, Johannes (1982), "Aspekte der Stadt im altindischen Staatslehrbuch des Kautilya" in: H. Kulke et al. (eds.), *Städte in Indien*, Wiesbaden.

Pieper, Jan (1982), "The Mofussil Environment: Elements of colonial Architecture in Up-country India", in: H. Kulke et al. (eds.), *Städte in Indien*, Wiesbaden

Rothermund, Dietmar (1978), "The Coalfield – An Enclave in a Backward Region", in: D. Rothermund and D.C. Wadhwa (eds.), *Zamindars, Mines and Peasants. Studies in the History of an Indian Coalfield and its Rural Hinterland,* New Delhi.

Rothermund, Dietmar (1980), "Epilogue: Urban Growth and Rural Stagnation", in: D. Rothermund et al. (eds.), *Urban Growth and Rural Stagnation. Studies in the Economy of an Indian Coalfield and its Rural Hinterland,* New Delhi.

Rothermund, Dietmar (1992), *India in the Great Depression, 1929-1939*. New Delhi.

Weber, Max (1964), *Wirtschaft und Gesellschaft*. Köln

4

Individual and Group Rights in Western Europe and India

Introduction: The Problem of Defining and Guaranteeing Group Rights

In order to do justice to the complex subject of this paper we shall start with a discussion of fundamental issues which can be traced to the deliberations of the respective committees of the United Nations. Their attempts at defining the problems concerned will help us to approach the rather different ways in which group rights were formulated in Western Europe and in India. The main causes for the formulation of such rights in Europe were the two world wars which affected the boundaries of nation states. Territorial minorities included in states dominated by national majorities had to be protected. In recent times the integration of immigrant communities has added a new dimension to European history in this respect. When turning to India we shall see that neither territorial nor immigrant communities are the major problem, but the broad spectrum of religious and linguistic minorities which are distributed all over the country. The world wars and their impact on national boundaries were of no consequence for India, but the colonial legacy and the partition of British India which exacerbated the disease for which it was supposed to be the cure made a deep impact on the construction of group rights in that country. Although the historical contexts are very different, the main principles governing group rights everywhere are, of course, the same, because modern legal thought is universalist in its scope. Actually, one of the more general aspects of this paper is the study of the encounter of universal principles with particular interests which becomes evident in every case to be discussed here. We shall return to this aspect at the end of this paper. To begin with we may refer to the basic dilemma of individual versus group rights which has perplexed many legal luminaries.

Modern legal thought attributes rights and duties to individuals rather than to groups. Thus the constituent individual members of a group are addressed in legal texts and not the group as such. A classical example is Article 27 of the International Covenant on Civil and Political Rights which asserts:

"In those States in which ethnic, religious or linguistic minorities exist, persons belonging to such minorities shall not be denied the right, in community with the other members of their group, to enjoy their own culture, to profess and practise their own religion, or to use their own language." (Capotorti 1978: iii)

The rights mentioned here are guaranteed to "persons" not to the "group". Francesco Capotorti, who wrote a learned report on "the rights of persons belonging to ethnic, religious and linguistic minorities" for the United Nations, commented on this aspect very explicitly:

".. the freedom of each individual member of a minority to choose between voluntary assimilation with the majority and the preservation of his own distinctive characteristics might be disregarded by the organs of the entity formed by the minority group, in its concern to preserve the unity and the strength of the group." (Capotorti 1978: 35)

But he also admits:

"... the rights in question will be exercised by the holders 'in community with the other members of their group' ... it is the individual as a member of a minority group, and not just any individual, who is destined to benefit from the protection granted by article 27". (Capotorti 1978: 36)

Thus we are faced with a typical "chicken or egg"-problem. Who comes first – the community which defines the characteristics of those who belong to it, or the individuals who make up this community? The assertion that "not just any individual" is to be protected by the Covenant concerned would focus on the community as a definitive entity, but the emphasis on the freedom of choice expressed earlier would highlight the priority of individual rights. Seen from this point of view, a community is freely constituted by the individuals who wish to belong to it. A commentator has stressed this by stating: "Respect for group rights does not justify group determinism'" and he has also emphasised that "the minority does not mediate between the individual and the state; it has no rights as such to preserve its identity". (Thornberry 1991: 394, 176)

In this context we should mention the difference between group rights granted to minorities and the right of self-determination guaranteed to "all peoples" by Article 1 of the United Nations Human Rights Covenant. Most states have argued, that this does not apply to minorities within independent states. In fact, India has contributed one of the most strongly worded statements of this kind:"... the words "the right of self-determination"... do not apply to sovereign independent States or to a section of the people or nation." (Thornberry 1991: 214)

At the time when this covenant was debated, Germany and India were opposed to each other as far as the emphasis on self-determination was concerned. Germany strongly advocated self-determination in view of the subjection of East Germany to Communist rule. India looked at self-determination from an entirely different perspective, because it was concerned with maintaining national unity. As we shall see later on, the right of self-determination is usually invoked by secessionists. When colonialism was still rampant, this right was, of course, meant to establish the claim for freedom of subject nations. But once these nations had become independent they jealously guarded their national integrity. When granting group rights to minorities they would thus agree with the statement that "the minority does not mediate between the individual and the state". Because once such "mediation" is accepted, the minority may soon graduate to the rank of a "people" and then stake a claim for self-determination.

In keeping with this denial of "mediation" the legal

construction of minority rights is based on the voluntary support of the individuals for their respective communities. This emphasis on the free will of individuals implies that the problem of excommunication is disregarded as it is related to "group determinism" which is not admissible. However, groups may wish to expel those individuals whose conduct violates their norms. From Capotorti's arguments quoted above we can see that he is concerned with the freedom of choice of the individual who may wish to leave the group, but he does not mention the problems of those who are deprived by the group of rights which they have hitherto enjoyed (e.g. sending their children to community schools, using community lands etc.) To whom do they appeal? In Europe no leading case seems to have settled this issue. For India there is a controversial Supreme Court judgement of 1962 which confirmed the right of the head of the Muslim Bohra community to excommunicate members of this community as he could otherwise not control it. This, of course, does not help those who may wish to challenge their excommunication.

Law suits concerning the exclusion from group rights can also arise if the state has ventured to define such rights by special legislation which deprives individuals from enjoying such rights if they do not meet the legal criteria. There are two interesting cases in which individuals have sued their respective state because legislation passed in order to protect a specific minority actually deprived them of their individual rights by giving priority to group rights. In one case (Lovelace v. Canada) a Canadian Indian woman who had married a non-Indian man had in doing this forfeited her right to live in the reservation allocated to her tribe. She argued that Indian men married to non-Indian women did not forfeit their rights in this way. The state replied that traditionally patriarchal relationships were taken into account in determining such legal claims. The Human Rights Committee of the United Nations quoted Article 27 mentioned above and supported the plaintiff. (Thornberry

1991: 207-210) In the other case (Kitok v. Sweden) a member of the Sami tribe sued the state which had defined the special rights of this tribe in terms of the profession of herding reindeer and excluding those who had not practised this for three years. The plaintiff had stopped herding reindeer for three years but wanted to return to this profession and was now debarred from enjoying the respective tribal rights. The Committee concluded that the state had tried to define the rights of the tribe in the interest of that community, but pleaded that the plaintiff should nevertheless be admitted to his past privileges – "albeit not of right". (Thornberry 1991: 211-213) These cases show the difficulties of applying the principles of Article 27 when dealing with specific legislation determining group rights.

Since only specific state legislation can define group rights, the states concerned need some guidance with regard to the definitions which they should embody in their laws. The crux of the problem is that of defining the term "minority". Legal scholars advising the United Nations have made valiant attempts at trying to define this term in precise legal categories which are universally applicable. Most scholars agree that Capotorti came closest to an acceptable definition:

"A group numerically inferior to the rest of the population of the state, in a non-dominant position, whose members – being nationals of the State possess ethnic, religious or linguistic charateristics differing from those of the rest of the population and show, if only implicitly, a sense of solidarity, directed towards preserving their culture, traditions, religion or language." (Capotorti 1978: 96)

Two terms in this definition deserve special attention: "nationals" and "implicitly". The first term restricts the operation of Article 27 to the citizens of a state. Resident foreigners do not require minority protection as their rights are defined by other articles of international law. (Thornberry 1991: 170) The second term points to the observable behaviour of the group concerned. The group does not need to manifest its existence by public declarations in order to be recognised as such.

Because of the emphasis on citizenship, Capotorti does not comment in detail on potential claims of minorities that culture and religion imply special laws of marriage and inheritance etc., since all citizens are usually subject to a unified civil code and minority rights pertain only to such matters as education, worship etc. He states that "the preservation of legal traditions of minorities in the field of private law is impeded by the trend towards applying a uniform set of rules to all nationals." He then refers to customary law in Africa and Asia and to the Gypsies in Europe, but he merely reports this and does not pass any judgement on these phenomena. (Capotorti 1978: 67) With regard to rights pertaining to marriage, he restricts his report to the various ways of concluding legally valid marriages among minority communities, but he does not go into the rights of divorce and inheritance which may be derived from the laws governing marriage. He only mentions that "... efforts undertaken to modify or eliminate certain customs which are regarded by the central government as obsolete in a modern state are reported to have met (with) limited success." (Capotorti 1978: 71)

In general he avoids discussing primordial ties as constitutive elements of minority identity. Most communities in question – unless they are sects or other proselytising groups – consist of members who are born as such. The guarantee of a "birthright", however, would be diametrically opposed to the very idea of fundamental rights which aim at non-discrimination and therefore cannot refer to inherent qualities of individuals which distinguish them from others. Article 27 quoted above could also be read as a plea for non-discrimination: persons who wish to preserve a specific form of culture, religion or language should not be discriminated against for doing so. But if non-discrimination is the only aim of Article 27, it would be redundant as that principle is enshrined in other articles of the respective covenant.

The rather weak wording of Article 27 which only stipulates that "rights should not be denied" could lead to the conclusion that it obliges the state only to abstain from discrimination. Therefore Capotorti deliberately stressed the obligation of the state to provide active support to the minorities: "In order to give effect to rights set forth in article 27... active and sustained measures are required from the States. A purely passive attitude on their part would render those rights ineffective." (Capotorti 1978: 99) But this implies the transition from non-discrimination to positive or protective discrimination. How can this be reconciled with the basic idea of equality which inspires all fundamental rights? The legal argument which tries to reconcile equality with protective discrimination stresses that the latter is only a means to achieve equality: "... the purpose of these (protective) measures is to institute factual equality between members of the minority group and other individuals."(Capotorti 1978: 41) Unfortunately, Article 27 as such does not make this type of interpretation mandatory. It can only be argued that the article would be superfluous if Capotorti's plea is rejected. A commentator has stated that other authors have given scant attention to this plea, and that many states have also tended to ignore Capotorti's argument (Thornberry 1991: 181). As we shall see, this is not plain negligence but reflects a crucial problem.

The need for the active support of the state and the fact that group rights can only be defined by legislation raises the question why states should feel obliged to pay attention to group rights at all and thus shoulder a heavy burden. Actually some states simply deny the existence of minorities on their territory or argue that those which do exist do not need to be protected in terms of group rights. On the other hand, among those states which do take such rights into account, we may find different political motives for this decision. Some of them may have been forced to acknowledge such rights due to international treaties which they had to sign. Others have guaranteed such rights in order to promote internal peace. Majority parties in some states may have cultivated minorities as voters so as to stabilise the political system. Of course, such motives are rarely discussed in public. An assertion of the adherence to international norms in this field will always be preferred. Legal debates will be conducted along such lines. But the historian will also be interested in the underlying motives. This kind of analysis will be pursued when we now turn to the regional accounts concerning Western Europe and India.

The Emergence of Minority Rights in Western Europe

After the end of the First World War the victorious powers established the League of Nations and under its auspices they tried to protect the rights of territorial minorities which had come under the jurisdiction of different nation states. An added sense of urgency was provided by the fact that these nation states had become democracies whereas they had earlier been ruled by monarchs who were at best quasi-constitutional. Monarchs have their own ways of dealing with minorities. They do not protect them in terms of abstract rights but special favours. Democracies are ill at ease when dealing with minorities as they are wedded to the ideology of national sovereignty and the social contract by which all citizens in their individual capacity jointly support the nation state. The "general will" implied by this ideology is disturbed by group rights granted to minorities. (Offe 1998: 189-193)

The two European powers which won the war, Great Britain and France, where actually no paragons in the field of minority rights. Their nation states had emerged over centuries of incessant struggle of a central power against regional interests. In France the Revolution had added to this assertion of a general (national) will. In fact, as late as 1977 the French government made the following straightforward statement:

"(France) cannot recognise the existence of ethnic groups, whether minorities or not. As regards religions and languages – other than the national language – ... these two areas form part, not of public law, but of the private exercise of public freedoms of citizens." (Capotorti 1978: 13)

In referring to the great diversity of local dialects, the French government asserted that they cannot be adapted to the development of ideas and techniques and are incapable of serving beyond their limited framework, thus they cannot be considered a necessary and sufficient element to define a community as opposed to the French nation.

The British government at the same time did not state its views in such categorical terms, but simply reported: "There is no general procedure for granting official recognition of minority groups in the United Kingdom as a means of safeguarding their rights since they exist without such recognition."(Capotorti 1978: 13)
In spite of this indifference of the French and the British to minority rights at home, they had imposed after the First World War – together with their allies – a series of treaties on other European states in which minorities rights were specifically guaranteed. The first treaty of this kind was that signed with Poland on 28 June 1919. (Thornberry 1991: 399 Appendix I) It served as a model for those concluded with a host of other states in the subsequent months of 1919. In the peace treaty imposed upon Germany at Versailles, however, there were no provisions concerning minority rights. This was, of course, due to the fact that Germany had lost rather than gained territories. But Germany took an initiative of its own and by Article 113 of the Weimar Constitution obliged the government to protect ethnic and linguistic minorities. This was not done for altruistic reasons but with a view to move the League of Nations to ensure that similar rights would be granted to German minorities abroad. The only recognised ethnic minority in Germany which benefited from this German initiative were the Sorbs or Wends who speak a Slavonic language and live around Bautzen and Cottbus in Eastern Germany. After the Second World War

the former German Democratic Republic revived the special cultural and educational group rights granted to these people. (Capotorti 1978: 63) These rights have been preserved after the re-unification of Germany. After the Second World War the Federal Republic of Germany had also concluded a treaty (1955) with Denmark of a reciprocal kind concerning the rights of the Danish minority in Germany and the German one in Denmark. (Capotorti 1978: 58,78) This mainly referred to the right of maintaining schools and the use of the respective languages. There are also some special arrangements of a political kind. German election laws stipulate that parties which do not get at least 5 per cent of the votes cannot be represented in the legislature. This provision does not apply to the Danish minority area of South Schleswig which is always represented by one member elected by the South Schleswig Voters Association.

Austria has granted minority rights to members of Slovenian and Croatian ethnic groups residing in its provinces of Carinthia, Burgenland and Styria. This has been re-confirmed by the Austrian State Treaty of 1955. On the other hand, Austria faced a problem concerning a substantial minority of people of Austrian origin residing in the Bolzano province of Italy where they constitute the majority of the population. This area, also referred to as Southern Tyrolia, had been ceded to Italy in 1919. Italy had promised to grant regional autonomy to this area, but this promise was not kept. Under fascist rule the people of this area were even forced to adopt Italian family names so as to eradicate any public trace of their identity. After Germany had annexed Austria in 1938, the German government entered into negotiations with Italy and arrived at a compromise: Members of the minority could opt for German citizenship and would then be resettled elsewhere in Germany. Many did this, but before they could be resettled, the Second World War had ended and Austria was revived. A peace treaty between Austria and Italy was signed in 1947; in this the minority was officially recognized. Families who wished to do so could revive their former names. This also applied to place names. In addition, the respective province was granted partial autonomy and legislative and administrative powers. (Capotorti 1978: 30) But the Italian government stacked the cards against the minority by designing the province in such a way that it included more Italians than members of the minority. The Austrian Chancellor, Bruno Kreisky, then appealed to the United Nations which passed two resolutions on this issue in 1960 and 1961. The provincial boundaries were then redesigned. The tortuous course of the history of this territorial minority illustrates almost all the problems which may arise when attempts are made to secure group rights in terms of regional autonomy. This kind of autonomy is certainly an appropriate means for protecting such rights if the respective minority inhabits a clearly defined territory.

The more important European examples of establishing minority rights by means of regional autonomy are Belgium and Switzerland. Belgium harbours two major and one minor linguistic groups, a French speaking, a Dutch (Flemish) speaking one and a small area inhabited by speakers of German. A delicate constitutional balance has been achieved by establishing three linguistic regions with equal rights and a fourth one consisting of the multilingual capital city Bruxelles. (Capotorti 1978: 110) Switzerland is a composite nation of a similar type. It has four major language groups: French, German, Italian and Romansh. All four languages are national languages and the respective populations have equal rights. German is the majority language (75 per cent), but this does not matter. The majority is not perceived as such. Switzerland consists of a large number of small administrative units called "cantons" which are autonomous to a very high degree. The population of most cantons is homogenous. (Capotorti 1978: 113)

Spain would also do well with similar arrangements, but before reverting to a democratic government under a constitutional monarchy it was for a long time subjected to a fascist dictatorship which exercised a strong central control. In recent years the Catalans have come to enjoy a large degree of regional autonomy in their province "Catalunya"(capital: Barcelona), but the Basques who are the other large linguistic minority group have some problems, because some of them fight for independence from Spain and thus are not easily contained in a federal structure. Secessionist movements of this type would also not like to be defined as a minority, because this would imply their recognition of a majority which grants rights to the minority. Such secessionists usually stress the right of self-determination to which we have referred above.

The spectrum of group rights in Western Europe is thus a very wide one. It ranges from composite nations in which a distinction between majority and minority does not really exist to such nation states in which some small minorities have been officially recognized and finally to states which refuse to think in terms of group rights at all. In recent times immigration has added a new dimension to the issue of group rights in Western Europe. The states of North and South America can argue that they are made up almost completely of immigrants. They insist on the rule that voluntary migrants have no claims to minority rights. In Europe the situation is different as some immigrant groups definitely constitute minorities. As long as they have not become citizens and only stay on as resident foreigners, they have no claims to minority rights as stated above. If they do become citizens and merge with the majority, they also do not claim minority rights. Great Britain has become a home for many people of its ex-colonies. But as indicated by the reply of the British government quoted above, the British are not inclined to think of granting anybody official minority rights, nor do the French who had to face a considerable influx of Algerians. Germany had invited many "guest labourers" in the 1970s, expecting that they would return to their home countries which many of them did not do. In addition, Germany attracted many people who made use of the liberal German laws concerning political asylum. It is rather difficult for foreigners to acquire German citizenship, and there are many foreign children born in Germany who would acquire citizenship automatically in other countries such as Great Britain, but have not yet become German citizens. The present German government wishes to reform the respective laws, even enabling immigrants to acquire dual citizenship (i.e. retaining also the citizenship of their countries of origin). This has become a contested issue on which the government and the opposition are deeply divided.

One point which actually has not been raised in this context is that once these immigrants become citizens they may claim minority rights. South European immigrants may not do so, but the largest group of immigrants are the Turks who are Muslims. Of course, even in their case the German government could point out that they are voluntary migrants and that this rules out any claim for minority rights. But would it be wise to follow this course or would it be better to grant them the rights to which ethnic, religious and linguistic minorities are entitled? The authorities of Berlin, a city with nearly one million Turkish inhabitants, has to deal with their claims even now, though most of them are not yet German citizens. German schools provide religious instruction for Catholics and Protestants and lessons in ethics for those who opt out of this denominational instruction. Turkish residents now demand Islamic instruction. This appears to be a reasonable request. It is actually endorsed by the German constitution which guarantees religious freedom. Although this is defined in terms of individual rights, the right "of unobstructed religious practice" which is specifically mentioned in the constitution would include communal worship, religious instruction etc. Religious instruction in schools is regulated by the provisions of Art. 7 of the German constitution. The state is entitled to supervise all schools. Religious instruction is defined as a regular subject to be taught in schools. Parents may decide about the participation of their children in the respective lessons. Religious instruction follows the principles defined by the religious communities. The constitution does not contain any statement concerning the teachers entrusted with religious instruction, except for the negative provision that no teacher can be compelled to teach this subject. But it is obviously taken for granted that the rights defined by the constitution entitle the respective community to appoint teachers responsible for religious instruction and to determine the syllabus and curriculum in this field. In the case of the Turkish minority this creates some problems. The Islamic association which has instituted a court case in Berlin in order to force the school authorities to provide Islamic instruction is known to be affiliated to a right wing Turkish political party. Turkish congregations in Berlin are organised as registered associations under German law. But their internal organisation is of a very autocratic kind; the Imam is in total control of the congregation on which he is imposed by the central organisation. The liberal provisions of the German constitution may thus be used so as to subject the religious institutions of the Turkish minority to autocratic control. Even if the German government does grant group rights to the Turkish minority and could then regulate such rights by legislation, this would not enable it to interfere with the religious practices of this minority. This example shows that guarantees of fundamental rights restrict the state in the construction of group rights.

Group Rights in India

India's experience with modern group rights in the public sphere began with the introduction of separate electorates for Muslims in 1909. This kind of rights did not exist in Europe unless one thinks of the differential franchise granted to various classes of the population in a number of European countries in earlier times. A restricted franchise based on property qualifications was also introduced in British India, but separate electorates were an additional boon granted by the colonial rulers. They were supposed to protect the large Muslim minority against oppression by the Hindu majority. Actually such a threat could only be envisaged in a system of parliamentary democracy and responsible government, but not under the Government of India Act of 1909 according to which the executive was still completely controlled by the Viceroy and the legislature had very limited functions. In such a system separate electorates appeared to be innocuous and even the liberal Congress leader, G.K. Gokhale, had no objections. However, when a step towards responsible government was made at the time of the next constitutional reform enshrined in the Government of India Act of 1919, separate electorates for Muslims proved to be dysfunctional. In their joint report the Viceroy, Lord Chelmsford, and the Secretary of State for India, Edwin Montagu, stated this explicitly, but also admitted that they could not abolish them now as the Muslims had come to look upon them as a precious right.

Indian political opinion other than that represented by the Muslim League tended to see the separate electorates in the same light as Chelmsford and Montagu. Nationalist politicians saw the alternative to this type of group rights in the inclusion of fundamental rights in the next constitution. When the All-Parties Conference chaired by Motilal Nehru presented a draft constitution in 1928 which was then referred to as "Nehru Report", it did away with separate electorates but contained a catalogue of fundamental rights. Against this M.A. Jinnah on behalf of the Muslim League repeated the claim for group rights in his famous Fourteen Points. The clash between fundamental rights and group rights dominated all further political debates in India. In its annual session of 1931 the Indian National Congress passed a long resolution, the "Karachi Resolution", with which it endorsed the claim for fundamental rights. The resolution contained a long list of such rights. As we shall see later on, this was looked upon as the heritage of the Indian freedom movement which had to be embodied in the constitution of independent India.

Although the British should have taken note of the

strictures passed on separate electorates by Chelmsford and Montagu, they even tried to protect the special interests of the Untouchables by such a measure in the next round of constitutional reforms. The British Prime Minister Ramsay Macdonald based his "Communal Award" on this system, but he kept the door open for a compromise to be arrived at by the respective parties in India. After Mahatma Gandhi's "Epic Fast" of 1932, Dr. B.R. Ambedkar accepted on behalf of the Untouchables the replacement of separate electorates by the reservation of seats. Gandhi made this more acceptable to Ambedkar by offering more reserved seats than those to which the Untouchables would have been entitled under the system of separate electorates. Moreover, the candidates for such seats would be selected in "primaries" in which only Untouchables could vote. But in the actual elections the candidates would have to secure a majority of votes in general electorates. For the candidates this meant that unlike those in separate electorates who could pose as ardent champions of the minority, they had to show a moderate profile and appeal to the electorate at large. Of course, it also meant that candidates supported by the National Congress would have a much better chance than those running for a party sponsored by Untouchables only. The National Congress broadened its social base in this way, whereas the Muslim League had to confine itself to Muslims in their separate electorates. But it could not prevent that other parties would also put up Muslim candidates for those separate electorates. This is what happened in the elections of 1936/37. Jinnah was deeply humiliated by the election results and could only hope to recover lost ground by adopting a more radical communal position. This he did with the Lahore Resolution of the Muslim League in 1940 which was accompanied by his speech in which he proclaimed the "Two Nations Theory".

With this theory Jinnah shifted his political base from that of a defender of group rights in Muslim minority provinces to that of a pleader for self-determination in terms of the autonomy of the Muslim majority provinces.

The logical outcome of this plea was secessionism, but Jinnah obviously hoped to retain his hold on the Muslim minority provinces while at the same time posing as a spokesman for the Muslim majority provinces. By insisting that the Muslim League was the sole representative of the Indian Muslims he also claimed that type of "mediation" which as we have seen above cannot be accepted by the state. However, the British-Indian state did accept this "mediation" in order to ward off the Indian claim for self-determination. In this way the Gordian knot was tied which then could only be cut by the partition of India.

The Constituent Assembly which had actually started to work before partition and then continued its deliberations under the impact of that tragic event, tried its best to build a strong foundation for the Indian nation by adopting a comprehensive catalogue of fundamental rights. In doing this it had to cover new ground as the existing constitution in keeping with British tradition did not contain fundamental rights at all. The Karachi Resolution of 1931 was taken as a blueprint, but whereas this resolution had been a good plank in an agitational platform, it was not suited for straightforward translation into a constitutional text. It contained social rights which the new state could aspire to, but could certainly not guarantee immediately without going bankrupt. Accordingly the catalogue was divided into justiciable fundamental rights and non-justiciable ones called "Directive Principles of State Policy".

Some important articles concerning group rights were actually included in the first category while it would have been more convenient to include them in the second one and leave the details to specific legislation of the kind which we have encountered when discussing group rights above. The Indian option for enshrining general articles concerning group rights in the fundamental rights catalogue of the constitution practically precluded the strategy of dealing with them by specific legislation. This put the burden of regulating the details on the courts. Whenever the courts were at the end of their tether, some problems could only be solved by legislation – but then of a very specific kind. We may refer to the articles of the constitution as first level legislation, the specific legislation mentioned above as second level legislation, and very specific laws such as the "Muslim Women (Protection of Rights on Divorce) Act, 1986" as third level legislation.

The first level legislation in trying to avoid the need for a second level one does in fact contain many elements which go beyond the statement of general principles and spell out group rights in some detail. In some instances the assertion of non-discrimination of the first parts of the respective articles is subsequently qualified so as to sanction group rights. Thus Article 16 (3) stipulates that officebearers of religious or denominational institutions may have to be members of the particular religious group and this inspite of the guarantee of equality of opportunity and non-discrimination mentioned in sections (1) and (2) of this article. Article 25 (1) guarantees freedom of conscience and the right to profess, practise and propagate religion "subject to public order, morality and health". An explanation added to this article explicitly mentions the carrying of kirpans by Sikhs as "deemed to be included in the profession of Sikh religion", obviously in order to make sure that nobody can claim that carrying such weapons may pose a threat to public order. Article 26 after stating the same proviso concerning public order etc. guarantees the right of any religious denomination or section therefore to maintain religious or charitable institutions, to manage its own affairs in matters of religion , to acquire property and to administer it.

A very interesting article which guarantees group rights in rather sweeping terms is Article 29 (1) which grants the right to conserve their distinct language, script or culture to "any section of citizens". Dr. Ambedkar who drafted this article intentionally avoided the term "minority" in this context, because he felt that in a multi-lingual and multi-cultural state like India communities of migrants who are settled in regions other than that of their origin may wish to have such rights. He stated that such communities are not "minorities in the technical sense but nonetheless minorities in the cultural and linguistic sense", (Gangwal 1995: 43). Actually this article seems not to have been made use of to the extent that its generous wording may lead one to expect, probably due to the fact that "minorities" are not mentioned here. (Gangwal 1995: 157) By contrast Article 30 (1) starts with the words "all minorities, whether based on religion or language..." and then proceeds to give them the right to establish and administer educational institutions of their choice. Since the aims mentioned in Article 29 (conserving language etc.) are not referred to in Article 30, the crucial term "of their choice" enables the minorities to run any type of educational institutions and making a handsome profit in doing so. Moreover, as Article 30 (2) stipulates, the state may not discriminate against minority educational institutions in granting aid to them. This generous provision of minority rights in the field of education has attracted the jealousy of the majority community which cannot establish similar institutions "of its choice". Article 29 does not provide an alternative to the majority community, because in it the aims of education are much more narrowly circumscribed. This has led to the strange situation that sometimes Hindu religious groups have tried to claim a sectarian minority status so as to be able to run institutions "of their choice".

Those who have heard about Aligarh Muslim University and Banaras Hindu University would perhaps think that both of them are institutions established by religious communities as "institutions of their choice", but this is not so. Both universities owe their existence to specific acts of the British Indian legislature and thus they are state universities in spite of their names. India's present constitution would not permit the state to establish universities which carry communal names, but as they did exist they continued to do so and the respective acts were even amended in independent India without changing the names of the universities. (Gangwal 1995: 160-163)

The fundamental rights enshrined in the constitution also contain articles establishing the principle of "protective discrimination" for the Scheduled Castes and Scheduled Tribes. In providing for this kind of positive discrimination the framers of the Indian constitution anticipated Capotorti's argument mentioned above. In this field there has been copious second level legislation covering special measures for the benefit of these disadvantaged minorities. Since all such measures are aimed at leading to equality rather than taking it for granted, they are not compatible with articles defining fundamental rights in term of equality and non-discrimination. Therefore the principle of positive discrimination had to be enshrined in the constitution. Nevertheless, some of the measures such as reservation of jobs etc. have been contested by those who felt deprived of opportunities in this way.

The most contentious issue in the field of group rights concerns the differences in private law. Constitutional law forms the basis of public law, and many lawyers and judges tend to feel that private law is distinct from public law and that it is wise to respect this division. In fact, in a leading case the Supreme Court explicitly rejected the relevance of constitutional provisions for a complicated case in which the right of succession to the headship of a Hindu religious institution was at stake (Conrad 1998: 214-215). Such cases may be rather recondite, a much more contentious field has been that of Muslim private law, particularly that pertaining to marriage and divorce. Strangely enough, Muslims argue that unlike Christians and Hindus who regard marriage as a sacrament they look upon the marriage contract as something not concerned with religion at all. Nevertheless, they insist on the observance of Islamic law in this field and are opposed to the introduction of a unified civil code for all citizens of India. The adoption of such a code has been re-commended in the Directive Principles of State Policy. Judges have occasionally referred to this recommendation and have urged Parliament to pass the respective legislation. The BJP has promised to do something about it in its election manifesto, but while in office it has also been reluctant to grasp this nettle. This may be due to the lack of the required majority and the dependence on coalition partners.

The multiplicity of private law in India becomes even more complex due to the fact that state legislatures may also contribute to what we have termed third level legislation. In this context the definition of "domicile" is of crucial importance, because state legislation is confined to those who reside in the respective state. This is actually in conflict with constitutional law which guarantees equal rights to all Indian citizens. Therefore Indian judges are careful not to refer to fundamental rights when dealing with private law, because an appeal to such rights could easily ruin the whole fabric of Indian private law. Numerous rules enshrined in Indian group rights are by their very nature clearly discriminatory (Otto 1996: 101-102). There is only one small and narrow "secular" path which leads through the jungle of group rights in this field and that is marked by the Special Marriage Act, 1954, for which people can opt if they do not want to be subject to their "communal" laws (Otto 1996: 103-104). Of course, the so-called "Hindu Code" has been reformed by legislation introduced in Jawaharlal Nehru's time. In this way Hindu law has been "modernised" to a large extent. But, of course, this is no substitute for a unified civil code, because the Hindu Code also refers to group rights – albeit of the majority.

The Islamic law pertaining to marriage and divorce is heavily biassed in favour of men and against women. It is therefore incompatible with the fundamental rights enshrined in the constitution. But as stated above, whosoever wants to refer to fundamental rights when dealing with groups right in the field of private law is anyhow treading on dangerous ground. The matter becomes even more complex, however, when officers of the state are obliged by legislation to enforce inequitable provisions. The Muslim Women (Protection of Rights on Divorce)

Act, 1986 is a case in point. This act was passed in order to solve a problem which arose due to a suit for maintenance by Shah Bano, a Muslim lady. As there was no remedy in Islamic law for her claim, the Supreme Court established her right to maintenance by referring to a purely "secular" law which is supposed to protect women from destitution and thus from becoming a burden for the public (Conrad 1998: 225-226). Muslim orthodox opinion regarded this judgement as interference with Islamic law. The Government of India caved in and Parliament then passed the act mentioned above. If one reads this act, one is surprised to see that the magistrate is supposed to follow the letter of Islamic law without having the chance to correct any injustice. A crucial item in the Muslim marriage contract is the pledge of a certain sum as compensation for the termination of this contract by the husband. Nowadays this is usually a rather symbolic amount which would hardly suffice for a few weeks of the divorced wife's maintenance. The magistrate only has to ascertain whether this amount has been paid, he cannot pass judgement on the amount however insufficient it may be. If the divorced wife cannot subsist on this amount, he has to check the whole gamut of her relatives who may have a duty to support her. Finally he has to turn to the Waqf Board, i.e. an Islamic charitable trust, in order to get some money for her. On no account may he approach the husband who has terminated the marriage contract. In other words, the provisions of the act place the magistrate in a rather humiliating position- and one may say that the state as such is humiliated in this way. The only remedy short of subjecting Muslims to a unified civil code is an amendment of the act which permits judicial determination of the amount of compensation to be paid. If Islamic opinion has supported the scheme according to which the magistrate must look into all these matters, it cannot really object to judicial determination either.

After surveying some of the problems concerning the granting of group rights in India, we may turn to the question raised earlier with regard to the political motives behind what has been done and what has not been done in this field. As has been pointed out the colonial device of separate electorates provided a powerful motive for replacing this dangerous group right by inserting fundamental rights into the constitution. The experience of partition had then added further emphasis to this quest. Moreover, the partition had by no means divided Jinnah's "two nations" properly, India was left with a large Muslim diaspora. In 1950 India and Pakistan concluded a treaty in which they assured each other that they would guarantee to the minorities throughout their territories complete equality irrespective of religion etc. (Capotorti 1978: 30) The terminology used was the same one as that in the catalogue of fundamental rights of the Indian constitution. There were, however, some more specific points mentioned, e.g. the rights of the members of the respective minorities to serve in the civil service and the armed forces etc. Furthermore, refugees had to apply for compensation to the state in which they had settled. This treaty seemed to provide an equitable solution for all problems arising from the partition of British India. Unfortunately it did not prevent the mass exodus of Hindus from East Pakistan prior to the emergence of Bangladesh. This was partly due to the fact that Pakistan turned into an Islamic state while Jinnah had thought of it as a secular state which guaranteed self-determination to is Muslim inhabitants. The more Pakistan stressed its Islamic identity, the more India insisted on secularism as its political philosophy. In keeping with this India was averse to dealing with groups rights by specific legislation in which the respective groups would have to be named and defined, but established such rights within the framework of fundamental rights.

In discussing political motives one must also mention how the majority election system worked in the Indian context. It was copied from British practice without much reflection. According to the textbooks of political science it invariably produces a two party system, but it did not do so in India. Instead it helped to maintain the "Congress system", i.e. the stabilisation of a centrist party by polarised opposition parties. Minority parties have no chance under such conditions. Under a different election law they could emerge as small parties which would form coalitions with bigger ones. But under the prevailing system, minorities could at the most provide "vote banks" for the ruling party. The Indian Muslims saw this point and the Congress leaders respected the rules of the game which meant that nothing should be done to offend Muslim opinion. The disadvantage of this informal agreement was that "Muslim opinion" remained a rather indeterminate phenomenon. A Muslim party would have had to spell out its aims, "Muslim opinion" does not need to do this. In fact, it remains powerful by letting others guess what it is all about. When crucial issues are at stake, the alarm raised by the most orthodox section of Muslim opinion is taken note of without asking how representative that section really is. Of course, in a truly secular state there should be no "communal" parties at all. Members of minorities should establish their political affiliations as individual citizens along the lines of social and economic issues. This is why India has insisted on fundamental rights rather than opting for a corporate state composed of various "communities".

In one respect, however, India has moved into the direction of a "group state". It has used Indian federalism and the rather flexible provisions of the Fifth and Sixth Schedules of the Indian Constitution in order to accommodate some minorities in terms of regional autonomy. Wherever such minorities occupy a clearly defined territory they could either be granted a federal state (e.g. Nagaland, Mizoram etc.) or a "scheduled area" with a large degree of autonomy. The latter was done for the Gurkhas of Darjeeling District where a "Darjeeling Gorkha Hill Council" was established in 1988. (Ghosh 1996: 16) Special problems arise where the respective minority is scattered and does not occupy a contiguous territority. The Bodos of Assam are a case in point. They have been granted a "Bodoland Autonomous Council" in 1993, but its territorial jurisdiction is rather vaguely defined as the area inhabited by the Bodos is not contiguous and there are large pockets of non-Bodos in this area. (Ghosh 1996:19) The Bodos are not yet satisfied with what they have got in this way. There is always the danger that the more radical among them may resort to "ethnic cleansing", driving out the non-Bodos who live in their midst.

The constitutional provisions which permit this type of accommodation are as follows: The First Schedule appended to the Indian Constitution contains a list of the federal states. This can be amended by Parliament and there are no limitations on the creation of new states except for the establishment of states for religious minorities as this would be repugnant to the idea of secularism. The Fifth Schedule ("Provisions as to the Administration and Control of Scheduled Areas and Scheduled Tribes") empowers the President of India to establish such areas and to define their borders (§6). This has proved to be a very flexible instrument for granting regional autonomy below the level of that enjoyed by a federal state. The Sixth Schedule pertains to Assam only. It empowers the Governor of Assam to establish autonomous districts and regions. Originally it was hoped that this would be sufficient for dealing with the claims of various tribes, but as the establishment of various small federal states in this region has shown, the provisions of the Sixth Schedule did not satisfy all of such claims. It should be added that all these provisions owe much to British colonial precedent. The Scheduled Districts Act of 1874 was a first step in this direction. The Government of India Act of 1919 included provisions concerning Backward Tracts, and the Government of India Act of 1935 listed Excluded and Partially Excluded Areas. Of course, the colonial rulers were more interested in securing the rights of the executive in such tracts rather than being concerned with regional autonomy. But this paved the way for accommodating regional interests in independent India.

Unlike group rights which are bestowed upon "persons", the grant of regional autonomy is of a different kind, because it is defined in territorial and not in personal terms. Persons benefit from it only as long as they are domiciled in the respective area, once they move out of it, they have no group rights of the type discussed earlier. In fact, the state may use the instrument of territorial autonomy in order to contain the proliferation of group rights of a more general kind.

Conclusion: Universal Principles and Particular Interests

The discussion of group rights has confronted us with the problem of finding a common denominator for universal principles and particular interests. We have seen that persons rather than groups are taken into consideration whenever the state guarantees group rights. But is is also admitted that persons enjoy such rights only in community with other members of their group. However, the group as such is not a legal entity. The recognition of its existence is based on its "implicit solidarity" not on the public claims made by those who pose as representatives of the group. The state as the guardian of universal principles such as the fundamental rights of all its citizens is the final arbiter when it comes to determining admissible interests of specific groups. The Swedish case concerning the Samis herding their reindeer has shown, that the state can go to great length in doing this. In recent times the United Nations have emerged as an umpire in this field, but their legal luminaries will side with the respective state if its legislation has been passed with the specific aim of protecting group rights. They will decide differently only when the state in determining group rights explicitly discriminates against women.

The duty of the state to protect the rights of women has by now become a universal principle which must be taken into consideration when dealing with particular interests. However, "customary law" in many parts of the world is based on patriarchal principles. This was cited in the case

Lovelace v. Canada mentioned above, but it is also obvious elsewhere. In order to cope with this problem a UN Convention on the Elimination of all Forms of Discrimination Against Women has been signed in 1980. The Government of India when signing this convention had added the proviso that with regard to marriage and family relations it will adhere to its policy of non-interference in the personal affairs of any community without its initiative and consent. But who will take the initiative? (Conrad 1998: 229) In view of what has been said about "Muslim opinion" above, there is hardly any chance that this particular community will take such an initiative under the prevailing conditions. Accordingly the state must see to it that the discrimination against women cannot be continued under the veil of private law. This is, indeed, a tall order, but as we have also seen above, the state is getting into a humiliating position when it not just tolerates discrimination but it is even obliged to support it by executive action.

The adherence to universal principles is not easy when dealing with group rights which refer to particular interests, the more so when we see that these principles must be enforced by the nation state. The French attitude mentioned above is the most forthright in this respect: the nation consists only of its citizens and cannot consider group rights at all. But most other nation states have not adopted this attitude and have granted group rights. It must be admitted that this is similar to the problem of squaring the circle. It can only be tackled by approximation. Thus universal principles must sometimes be stretched so as to accommodate particular interests, but this should not be done to the extent that these principles are completely subverted.

Acknowledgements: The author wishes to thank Dr. Dieter Conrad, Heidelberg, and Prof. Ulrich Spellenberg, Bayreuth, for comments on earlier drafts of this paper.

References:

Capotorti, Francesco (1978), *Study on the Rights of Persons Belonging to Ethnic, Religious and Linguistics Minorities*, United Nations, New York (UN Sales No.E.78.XIV.1)

Conrad, Dieter (1998), "Rule of Law and Constitutional Problems of Personal Laws in India", in: Satish Saberwal & Heiko Sievers, eds., *Rules, Laws, Constitutions,* New Delhi: Sage

Gangwal, Sunita (1995), *Minorities in India. A Study in Communal Process and Individual Rights*, Jaipur: Arihant

Ghosh, Partha S. (1996), *Ethnic Conflict and Conflict Management: The Indian Case*, Kandy (International Centre for Ethnic Studies)

Offe, Claus (1998), " `Homogeneity´ and Constitutional Democracy: Group Rights as an Answer to Identity Conflicts?" in: Satish Saberwal & Heiko Sievers, *Rules, Laws, Constitutions*, New Delhi: Sage

Otto, Dirk (1996), *Rechtsspaltung im indischen Erbrecht – Bedeutung und Auswirkung auf deutsch-indische Nachlaßfälle*, Frankfurt/M.:Lang

Thornberry, Patrick (1991), *International Law and the Rights of Minorities*, Oxford: Clarendon Press

5

India in World Affairs

From the perspective of 1997 South Asia appeared to be a relatively quiet place and accordingly it did not attract world attention. In general, South Asia catches such attention only off and on and the only remaining superpower, the United States of America, has rarely shown a consistent interest in this region. India, the major regional power, is interested in maintaining the status quo. Pakistan which used to be a "frontline state" until 1989 lost this position after the Soviet withdrawal from Afghanistan and the subsequent collapse of the Soviet empire.

Whereas comments on India in world affairs are often dominated by short term impressions, we shall try to take a long term view which would also enable us to identify trends which are of importance for future developments. In following this approach we shall first look at the unstable equilibrium which characterizes the relation between India and China. We shall then consider India's policy towards its immediate neighbours. Subsequently we intend to highlight the importance of South Asia's vast Muslim population. Last but not least we want to examine the relevance of Samuel Huntingdon's "Clash of Civilisations" for South Asia.

India and China – an Unstable Equilibrium

The rivalry between India and China became apparent even at the Asian Relations Conference convened by Nehru in 1947 as interim Prime Minister. He proclaimed at that time that Asia was a zone of peace which had only been disturbed by the colonial powers. Once they had withdrawn, peace would return to Asia. But even during this conference there was a tussle about the location of the permanent secretariat of the Asian Relations Conference. China was supposed to convene the second conference and wished to postpone the decision on the secretariat, hoping that it could then be set up in China. But Nehru finally succeeded in establishing it in New Delhi. However, due to the subsequent course of events he soon lost interest in it. The second conference could not be held in China where in the meantime the revolution had changed all timetables.

Nehru relied on the anti-imperialism of the Chinese revolutionaries. When they occupied Tibet in 1950, he did not object and immediately ceded the extra-territorial rights in Tibet which India had inherited from the British. In 1954 India and China concluded a border treaty which unfortunately did not specify the border but only mentioned some passes open for trade between India and Tibet. The treaty also included the five principles (*Panchshila*) of peaceful co-existence which Nehru repeatedly emphasized in subsequent years, but which did not mean anything to the Chinese.

The defence of the long Himalayan frontier was an impossible task for the Indian army. This border was neither delimited nor demarcated. The only strategy to be adopted against a Chinese invasion would be the cutting of supply lines wherever they would send their troops across the mountains. But the Chinese rather sliced off some pieces of Indian territory in a clandestine manner. When India became aware of this, there was an exchange of notes which Nehru did not publish so as not to excite public opinion. The Chinese built roads on Indian territory in Aksai Chin so as to complete a ringroad around the terrible desert Taklamakan. This ringroad finally connected Lhasa with Sinkiang via the Karakorum Pass. It then went on to China via Inner Mongolia and was thus an essential element of control of the outer regions of this huge state. It was only when the Dalai Lama fled to India in 1959 that the strained relations between India and China came into the limelight and Nehru could no longer avoid public criticism for his handling of the broader issue.

When Chou En-lai visited India in 1961 he did not wish to discuss such details with Nehru but suggested a deal:

China would recognize the McMahon line in the East if India would make concessions as far as the Karakorum area was concerned. Nehru could not make such concessions as he would have been criticized in Parliament for giving up Indian territory. The border war of 1962 then followed exactly the pattern of the suggested deal. A Chinese division crossed the McMahon line and came down to the Indian plains. But this spectacular attack was a diversionary move. The Chinese withdrew before their supply lines could be cut. In the Western sector, however, they advanced towards the Karakorum Pass and retained it. After this there was a conspiracy of silence on both sides. The Chinese kept quiet because they had got what they wanted and the Indian government did not wish to advertise its humiliating losses. Nehru had to accept the failure of his foreign policy. His health deteriorated and he died in May 1964.

The Indian army had lost its reputation due to this Chinese demonstration war and Pakistan felt encouraged to solve the Kashmir problem by force. It entered into an alliance with the victorious Chinese in 1963, but was disappointed when the new ally did not open a second front in the East during the war of 1965. Pakistan's defeat in this war led to the demand for autonomy in East Pakistan which culminated in the secession of Bangladesh in 1971. This development led to the emergence of India as the predominant regional power. In this way India also improved its standing with regard to China. But there was no immediate normalisation of the relations between India and China. Only the Janata government which came to power in 1977 took a new initiative. The Minister of External Affairs, Atal Bihari Vajpayee, visited China in 1979 for this purpose, but unfortunately China launched just at that time a demonstration war against Vietnam, a country which India had befriended for a long time. Deng Xiaoping added insult to injury by comparing the war against Vietnam to the border war with India in 1962. Both wars had the aim of teaching the enemy a lesson according to Deng's interpretation. Vajpayee left China immediately and the relations between the two major countries of Asia were once more at a low ebb.

After Indira Gandhi had returned to power in 1980, the Ministry of External Affairs tried to improve relations with China by keeping quiet on all areas of disagreement. But only Prime Minister Narasimha Rao succeeded in 1993 to normalize relations with China. Both sides signed a treaty in which they pledged to respect the line of actual control. This treaty was in some ways similar to that of 1954 which also did not specify the border in unambiguous terms. After signing this treaty Narasimha Rao frequently emphasized China's right to rule over Tibet even on occasions which did not call for such a statement. Whether India will really benefit from this kind of "political correctness" remains to be seen.

This "correctness" should not detract from the fact that India continued to look at China with some reservations. After all China is a nuclear power with rockets on the "Roof of the World" which could be aimed at targets in India. India never gave up its "nuclear option" and it was estimated in 1996 that India possessed about 200-300 kg Plutonium with which it could produce a big battery of atombombs. But, of course, it so far lacked a delivery system and the operational capacity of conducting a nuclear war. Therefore India preferred to pursue a policy of "nuclear ambiguity", keeping potential enemies guessing at India's state of nuclear preparedness.

India had successfully tested a rocket named "Agni" which was supposed to have a range of 2500 km, but the tests were restricted to 1000-1500 km. The production of these rockets was then stopped for some time, they were referred to as "technology demonstrators". India did not claim that this was a weapons system of operational quality. The smaller "Prithvi"-rockets with a reach of 250 km were, however, fully operational. The officers of the conventionally armed forces still tended to be sceptical about all those homemade rockets. There was so far no strategic concept with regard to the deployment of rockets. Nevertheless by 1997 India had at least one rocket regiment trained to deal with this new type of armament.

India could not forego the "nuclear option" and sign the NPT or the CTBT unless it would sign a pact with a nuclear power, providing it with a nuclear umbrella. This would have been against all principles of foreign policy observed by India so far. Moreover, it would not have been a practical possibility at all. A nuclear power providing such an umbrella would have to see an immediate advantage in doing so and it would also have to have the massive capacity to adopt a "protectorate" as huge as India. On the other hand, China did not refrain from supplying rockets to Pakistan and probably helping it in other ways, too. Earlier experiences had shown that China would not be willing to back Pakistan to the hilt. But China was obviously interested in supporting Pakistan as a regional counterweight to India. This kept India on tenterhooks – and, of course, it was meant to do just that. India on the other hand could not do the same thing to China.

India and its Neighbours: From the "Big Stick" to the Gujral Doctrine

India is surrounded by smaller neighbours which have no common borders among themselves, but all have some reason or the other to be apprehensive of India. For obvious reasons, India wished to prevent the neighbours from ganging up against it and therefore preferred to deal with them strictly on bilateral terms. India Gandhi was known as "the lady with the big stick" because of her insistence on this type of policy. Inder Kumar Gujral who had earlier been Minister of External Affairs and then became Prime Minister of India changed this line by adopting a policy of unilateral accommodation of India's neighbours. In this way he wanted to reconcile India's neighbours with the obvious preponderance of the region's biggest power. His way of relying on confidence building measures attracted the neighbours. This new policy guideline soon became know as "Gujral Doctrine" although he himself had never referred to it in those terms.

In a way this policy was a continuation of India's positive turn towards the SAARC-idea. Originally this idea which was sponsored by the President of Bangladesh, Zia-ur Rahman, was not received kindly by India. It was obviously aimed at replacing bilateralism at the time when Indira Gandhi had just returned to power in 1980. The South Asian summit proposed by Zia-ur Rahman could thus not materialize very soon, and as he was assassinated in 1981 he did not live long enough to see the implementation of his plan. Several preparatory meetings at various levels had to pave the way to the summit which was finally reached in 1985. But when the Government of Bangladesh hosted this meeting in Dhaka in 1985 it was surprised at the eagerness of the heads of government who wished to hold such summit meetings from now on every year whereas one had hoped at the most for a meeting every other year. The heads of government obviously noted the convenience of such meetings where all kinds of issues could be discussed informally beyond the rather limited agenda. Nowadays heads of government hardly ever meet unless the communique which is to emerge from their meeting is settled well in advance. Only state funerals usually provide opportunities for meetings without a communique. The other reason for welcoming annual meetings of the SAARC-type is that heads of government are frequently replaced due to coups or the results of elections. Thus there will always be new faces even at annual meetings.

The first SAARC-summit of 1985 took place at a time which was particularly conducive for such an initiative. The Soviet presence in Afghanistan was at its height. India was much affected by this just because it had to keep quiet so as not to disturb Indo-Soviet relations. Zia-ul Haq, the President of Pakistan, was at the zenith of his power as leader of a "front state" supported by the Americans. Rajiv Gandhi had scored many points during his first year in office and still seemed to be taking everything in his stride. President Ershad of Bangladesh who hosted this first summit was also still firmly in control of his state. All this did not last long. Zia died in a mysterious accident in 1988, Rajiv Gandhi lost the elections of 1989 and Ershad was overthrown soon after that. It is remarkable that in spite of all these events, the SAARC-summits were held almost always on time. There was only one hiatus between the fourth summit in 1988 and the fifth one in 1990 due to tensions between India and Pakistan in 1989.

While SAARC did make some progress, the security problems of South Asia which had been deliberately kept out of the SAARC agenda remained contentious. India had several times asserted its ability to intervene in regional affairs and, of course, it could not expect official approval of its neighbours for that. The President of the Maledives had reasons to be grateful to India, because an Indian military intervention in 1988 had saved him from a coup. But the dispatch of an Indian Peace Keeping Force to Sri Lanka in 1987 was a more problematic affair. Initially India had air-dropped food supplies for the Tamil rebels who were surrounded by the troops of the Sri Lankan government. Nepal reacted to this by ordering Chinese anti-aircraft guns and thus started a conflict with India which led to a blockade of this landlocked country some time later. The President of Sri Lanka, J.R.Jayewardene, reacted differently to India's intervention. He arrived at an accord with Rajiv Gandhi and invited the Indian Peace Keeping Force. Under this accord India was obliged to disarm the Tamil rebels whom it had supported earlier. This was a clever move on Jayewardene's part, but it became a very costly and humiliating affair for India. In due course several Indian divisions were stationed in Sri Lanka, but they did not succeed in disarming the rebels. Once more it was demonstrated that guerillas operating on their home ground are in a better position than a foreign occupation power. The Indian troops were perceived as such a power. Finally Jayewardene's successor Premadasa demanded a withdrawal of the Indian Peace Keeping Force and thus put an end to the legitimacy of its staying on in Sri Lanka. In the meantime Rajiv Gandhi had lost the elections and the new government withdrew the Indian troops unceremoniously. The venture had proved to be a painful lesson for India. Nevertheless, the Tamil rebels obviously feared that Rajiv Gandhi would intervene once more if he was returned to power. Therefore they assassinated him during an election tour of Tamil Nadu in May 1991.

India's clashes with Pakistan had been of a different kind. The wars of 1965 and 1971 had been conventional wars in which regular troops faced each other on the battlefield. India had won both wars, but it had not derived substantial benefits from that. After the first war, Pakistan had signed a treaty pledging that it would refrain from the use of force, after the second war it also signed a treaty which stipulated that all further conflicts between India and Pakistan should be settled bilaterally, i.e. without recourse to other countries or international organizations. Pakistan had then tried hard to circumvent these obligations. Since open warfare against India had led to disastrous results for Pakistan, it opted for indirect and clandestine measures, particularly in Kashmir which had been a bone of contention ever since the partition of British India.

There is an impression in Pakistan that India has never got reconciled to this partition. India has certainly accepted the territorial consequences of this partition, but it can never accept the principle on which it was based: Jinnah's two-nations theory. With its large Muslim minority India simply cannot subscribe to this theory, because it would have to recognize the Muslims living in India as foreign nationals and not as citizens. This is also the basic problem behind the Kashmir conflict. As a princely state, Kashmir was not partitioned like British India. When the Maharaja of Kashmir opted for the accession of his state to India, Nehru promised that a plebiscite would be held later on. He obviously did not realize at that time that the issue at stake in such a plebiscite would be whether Indian Muslims consider themselves to be foreign nationals who wish to join Pakistan or whether they feel that they are Indian citizens who should remain in India. The partition of British India was an administrative act of the British colonial rulers. It had not been accompanied by a plebiscite. A plebiscite in Kashmir would have raised the fundamental issue mentioned above for the first time – and it was bound to have an impact on India's Muslim citizens throughout the country. For this reason India refrained from ever holding this plebiscite while Pakistan continued to insist on it.

It is easy to fish in troubled waters in Kashmir by encouraging infiltrators who are variously described as indigenous "rebels" or "freedom fighters", but who were frequently recruited from among the militant tribes in the frontier region or even in Afghanistan. After the Soviet withdrawal from Afghanistan many of the Afghan *mujahedin* experienced in guerilla warfare shifted their activities to Kashmir and tied down large contingents of the Indian army and of the Border Security Force. Under such conditions it was no easy task to return to political normalcy in this tormented state.

Until the Kashmir conflict is settled by bilateral negotiations leading to a recognition of the so called "Line of Control" as international border, there will be no peace in South Asia. Pakistan has always aimed at parity with India. It cannot hope to achieve this in conventional terms. Only as a nuclear power Pakistan could claim parity with India. Whether this would then lead to an equilibrium of mutual deterrence is a moot point. Religious fanaticism on both sides could easily upset such an equilibrium.

South Asia's Muslims: The Majority of the Islamic World

Religious conflicts can end up in violent confrontations as the destruction of the Babri Masjid of Ayodhya by fanatical Hindus in 1992 has shown. In the meantime India has settled down to normal life once more. But such conflicts are endemic and could always flare up again. The population of South Asia consists at present of about 800 mill. Hindus and 330 mill. Muslims. The Hindus live mostly in India, whereas the Muslim population is more or less evenly shared by Bangladesh, India and Pakistan. The Muslims of South Asia are the majority of the Islamic world. The future development of this Islamic world will be determined to a large extent by what happens in South Asia. Islamic fundamentalism in its virulent form has not attracted much attention in South Asia where Islam is deeply enmeshed with regional folk traditions. The mysticism of the Sufis has contributed more to the spread of Islam in South Asia than the proverbial conversion by the sword. The Islamic scholars of South Asia have sponsored many schools of thought which each in their own way tried to reconcile Islamic tradition with modern ideas. This has given rise to a rich variety of thought which cannot be easily streamlined into a fundamentalist doctrine. But fundamentalism penetrates South Asia from the outside. The money of Saudi Arabia plays a great role in this respect. It is said that many fundamentalist intellectuals in charge of distributing this money are originally from South Asia.

Zia-ul Haq had subjected Pakistan to a campaign of "Islamisation from above", i.e. a state sponsored programme of streamlining Islamic education and religious practice. In this he did not necessarily win the support of traditional Islamic scholars who resent being turned into instruments of state power. The Islamic educational institutions which Zia supported by re-introducing *zakat,* a tax which must be spent on individual students in such institutions have in the meantime spawned a large number of graduates who could not find secular employment. Zia enhanced their frustrations by equating their degrees with those of secular colleges and universities. They accordingly felt that they should find jobs equivalent to those available to other students. Thus the *taliban* (=graduates of Islamic institutions) had to fend for themselves. Many of them had come from Afghanistan to Pakistan where they were welcomed by the heads of Islamic institutions who had to produce lists of names of students in order to qualify for *zakat* grants. On returning to Afghanistan after graduation, the *taliban* captured the state as this was the only way of finding gainful employment. Bangladesh has not yet been subjected to similar programme. It did insert the term "Islamic" in its constitution, but it did this mainly in order to please Saudi Arabia which has pumped much money into this poor country. However, this gesture was not accompanied by the measures which Zia introduced in Pakistan.

In India the idea of the secular state was interpreted in such a way as to leave the Muslims to their own devices as far as legal matters such as marriage and divorce, family property and inheritance are concerned. This was taking the line of least resistance and the National Congress could for a long time rely on the Muslim vote. Under the election laws prevailing in India, a Muslim party would never have a chance to win a seat. Moreover, the Muslims are a diaspora community in India. Except for Kashmir they are widely dispersed and there would be few constituencies in which they could muster any strength at all. But the Muslims are not only dispersed, there is also nothing like a class solidarity among them. They belong to many different walks of life. They nowhere form a society of their own, but are part and parcel of local society. The novel "*Ardha Gaon*" (Half the Village) by the Indian Muslim author Raza reflects this reality of Muslim life in India. It is interesting to note that the same author was commissioned to write the script for the television series on the Indian national epic *Mahabharata.* This is a hopeful sign of practical secularism in India. If this kind of atmosphere prevails, South Asian Islam will not succumb to an artificial fundamentalism.

At present there is a threat to this secular symbiosis from the rise of political Hindu traditionalism which is as artificial as the political fundamentalism of Islam. The new solidarity of the Hindus is essentially a reaction to modern Islamic fundamentalism, but it is also directed against the conservative Islamic orthodoxy which insists on the privileges of Muslims and rejects the idea of a uniform civil law. The orthodox Muslims are not fundamentalists, but if they feel threatened by the Hindus they may make common cause with the fundamentalists. This is a vicious circle which is very dangerous. Muslims interested in social reform who are neither close to the orthodoxy nor to the fundamentalists have a hard time under such conditions.

Hindu traditionalism was a potent force in the Indian freedom movement against British rule. This type of traditionalism is a modern ideology not to be confused with the adherence to living traditions. It opposed untouchability and the caste system in order to establish national solidarity. Indian monistic philosophy was quoted by these modern traditionalists so as to prove that all divisive tendencies in Hinduism belong to the realm of illusion. In confronting colonial rule, this was a convincing ideology. But after independence political organizations which tried to conjure up Hindu solidarity remained marginal. In recent years a more primitive traditionalism has been introduced which does not rely on philosophy but stresses more tangible symbols. The campaign which ended with the destruction of the mosque at Ayodhya was an object lesson of this kind.

The appeal of this cruder type of traditionalism increases with the impact of general secularization which diminishes the substance of genuine religiosity. The young middle-class Hindu who is as much influenced by television as his contemporaries elsewhere knows perhaps very little about the religious ideas of his ancestors, but he has seen the *Ramayana* on television and accordingly he has an image of King Rama in his mind. A campaign for rescuing his birthplace may therefore appeal to him – it feels like a continuation of the television series in real life. Rama never fought against Muslims as they did not exist in his times, he fought against demons. But if his birthplace is occupied by a mosque defended by Muslims, they can be "demonized". This kind of short-cut traditionalism is very dangerous. If it is instrumentalised for political purposes it can easily set South Asia ablaze.

The Indian army has so far remained loyal to secularism. Moreover, Muslims are adequately represented in this army. It is proud of its professionalism and of staying aloof from politics. But even such an army cannot remain isolated from currents which move the society at large. If tensions between Muslim fundamentalism and Hindu traditionalism increase, the army may one day be called upon to defend Hindu India against Islam. Under such conditions it would have to dismiss its Muslim soldiers. A militarised Hindu India would then look with hatred upon its Muslim neighbours and the wider circle of states such as Iran and the new republics which have emerged from the erstwhile Soviet Union. Seen from this perspective the events of India's internal politics may be of crucial importance for world affairs in general. The positive scenario which we could set against the terrible one mentioned above would be a democratic India which succeeds in keeping its internal peace and would thus have a stabilising influence on its Muslim neighbours. In this way India could check the advance of Islamic fundamentalism.

South Asia and the "Clash of Civilisations": A Terrifying Scenario

At a first glance our analysis of the security problems in South Asia seems to fit in well with the pattern of Samuel Huntingdon's "Clash of Civilisations". Huntingdon's book was an answer to Francis Fukuyama's "The End of History". With the end of the Soviet empire, Western universalism seemed to triumph and to encompass the whole world. Since history is a process of conflicts, the end of all conflicts in a unified world would also mean the end of history. Huntingdon argued against this that new conflicts are arising in terms of his "Clash of Civilisations". According to him there are only seven civilisations which really matter: the West, the Islamic world, the Russian-Orthodox one, China, Japan, Hindu India and black Africa. He says very little about the last two civilisations. His main protagonists are the West and the Islamic world. He realizes that civilisations cannot be actors on the world stage, therefore he identifies "core states" which act on behalf of the respective civilisations. The areas of conflict are marked by "fault lines" between neighbouring civilisations. China appears to him as a natural ally of the Islamic world, perhaps because there are no fault lines between them. The rivalry between India and China and China's alliance with Pakistan fit in well with this scenario, but Huntingdon does not comment on this. His main idea is to show that there are resistant civilisations which will not submit to Western universalism or support the hegemony of a Western dominated world order. This is certainly correct, but Huntingdon overstates his case by lapsing into a civilisational essentialism. Islamic fundamentalism fits in well with his thesis. But he must admit that there is no Islamic "core state". For China, on the other hand, he is somewhat at a loss about identifying its ideology. In earlier writings he mentioned "Confucianism", but Sinologists have dissuaded him from using this term and since then he refers to the "Sinic" civilisation. His "civilisations" are ideological constructs and this could be particularly dangerous if it turns into a self-fulfilling prophecy.

In the introduction to his book Huntingdon projects himself as a broad-minded scholar who acknowledges the variety of civilisations and criticizes Western hegemony, but actually his thesis is a typical Western attempt at designing a world order in which everything fits into a predetermined scheme. He is not at all interested in finding out how the other civilisations see themselves or others. If he is right, they have to conform to the pattern which he has discovered. At the end of his book he reveals his true intentions: he wants to strengthen American identity and he rejects multiculturalism. Other civilisations may exist outside the American framework, this is their rightful place, but there is no room for multiculturism within the country. This is a message of despair for all those who work for multiculturalism within existing states. The positive scenario for India which we have mentioned above would be doomed according to Huntingdon. If American political leaders would adopt Huntingdon's scheme as guideline for their future actions, this would be a terrible security risk for South Asia.

References:

Arnett, E. (ed.) (1997), *Military Capacity and the Risk of War. China, India, Pakistan and Iran*, Oxford

Banerjee, D.(1995), "Die Verteidigung", in: D. Rothermund (ed.), *Indien. Kultur, Geschichte, Politik, Wirtschaft, Umwelt. Ein Handbuch,* Munich

Huntingdon, S.(1996), *The Clash of Civilisations and the Remaking of World Order,* New York

The Fall-Out of a New Political Regime in India

The formation of a government led by the Bharatiya Janata Party (BJP) is certainly a new departure in Indian politics. All previous governments were formed either by the Indian National Congress or by politicians who had earlier belonged to that party. The BJP and its precursor the Bharatiya Jan Sangh had always been in the opposition with the exception of the brief interlude of the Janata government (1977-1980) in which the present Prime Minister, Atal Bihari Vajpayee, held the post of Minister of External Affairs. The BJP has consistently stood for Hindu nationalism and has attacked the secularism of the Congress as a spurious ideology which should be replaced by genuine secularism. The fact that the BJP is now in power should therefore signify the establishment of an entirely new regime in India.

"Regime" means a system of government. In terms of constitutional law India is a federal, democratic republic and there is no indication that the new party in power is going to change that. But the actual conduct of political affairs can vary a great deal within the general framework established by constitutional law. Political scientists used to refer to the "Congress system". This was characterised by the domination of a centrist party whose power was based on a polarisation of leftist and rightist forces which would help it to capture a majority of parliamentary seats. The Congress system excluded coalition politics, because once the Congress opted for a leftist or a rightist partner, it would forfeit its centrist position. As recent elections have shown, the Congress system has failed and an era of coalition politics has begun. In this new era the BJP had an initial advantage. It did not need to shy away from entering into coalitions. It held no centrist position as it was clearly a rightist party. But for this very reason it had to overcome the reluctance of potential partners who knew very well what it meant to subject themselves to the discipline imposed by the BJP. Thus the BJP projected a more moderate image, personified by Atal Bihari Vajpayee, who was frankly called a "convenient mask" by one of the party secretaries. The strategy worked and although the verdict of the electorate was not at all explicit, the BJP rose to power by taking on board a motley crowd of allies. Initially there was a feeling that these allies may constrain the policy options of the BJP in various ways. It seemed that the radical points of its programme, such as going nuclear, would have to be shelved. But the "BJP system" which has replaced the "Congress system" implies that allies soon become captives and are in no position to influence the policies of the major partner. Most of these allies have no particular principles to defend. If they leave the government they would soon be reduced to insignificance. It is only with regard to their respective regional power bases that they may be somewhat sensitive. This the BJP will respect while aiming at depriving them of such power bases in the long run. Taking this situation into consideration we may, indeed, speak of a new political regime in India.

For a closer analysis of the political situation in India we shall first have a look at the verdict of the electorate and then at the formation and composition of the government. Subsequently we shall discuss the policy options in internal and external affairs and the fate of economic liberalisation. The tests of atomic bombs in India and Pakistan will be discussed in this context.

The Uncertain Verdict of the Electorate

The elections of March 1998 repeated in general the outcome of the previous ones: they did not provide any party with a clear mandate to form a government. There was only one major difference between the results of 1996 and 1998 with regard to the position of the regional parties. They had emerged as a third force in 1996 and were able to form the "United Front"-government with the help of the Janata Party and the Communists and supported from the outside by the Congress. The weight of the parties which had participated in the United Front government was greatly reduced in the 1998 elections. This does not necessarily mean that the voters were so dissatisfied with that government that they wanted to defeat it by all means. But they were obviously annoyed by the way in which this government was brought down twice by the withdrawal of Congress support. In both cases the reasons for this withdrawal were not major policy issues but power struggles. The Congress did not gain much credit for this appalling conduct of political affairs, and seen in this light it should have done even worse in the elections than the parties of the unfortunate United Front, but it benefited from the polarisation which characterised the 1998 election. Actually elections under the system prevailing in India should automatically reduce the contest to two parties. This has so far not happened in India, because the Congress could always benefit from a three cornered fight in which right and left parties would cancel each others gains.

The 1984 elections were the last ones in which this worked in a most striking manner. In 1989 V.P. Singh spoiled this game by arriving at an electoral understanding with the BJP. He did not put up candidates of his Janata Party in constituencies where the BJP had good chances. In this way the Congress was beaten with a vengeance, but V.P. Singh could only form a minority government tolerated by the BJP on the one side and the Communists on the other. The old three cornered fight at election times was now replaced by a three cornered system of government support which depended on the mutual incompatibility of the two "tolerant" partners which kept the minority government in suspended animation. This unstable equilibrium collapsed when the BJP challenged the government. In the subsequent elections (1991) the BJP gained from this challenge and the Janata Party (JP) was badly defeated. But the Congress party also made some headway. The polarisation effect heralding the emergence of a two-party system seemed to be obvious. One could have expected that this trend would continue at the time of the next elections. But instead of this the regional parties came into the limelight. The BJP had become the strongest party and was accordingly invited by the President to form a government, but it was as yet unable to recruit a sufficient number of allies so as to form a coalition government.

Table 1: Distribution of Seats in the Indian Parliament (Lok Sabha) 1984-1998

Year	Seats (tot.)	Con-gress	BJP	JP	Cong. +BJP +JP	CPI	CPM	Oth.**
1984	515	405	2	10	81%	6	22	70
1989	529	197	86	142	80%	12	33	59
1991	495	220	117	54	79%	11	35	58
1996	537	136	160	43	63%	11	32	155
1998	547	141	179	1	58%	9	32	185

The numbers listed here refer to the seats for which valid election results were declared; in 1989 elections in Assam and in 1991 in Panjab had to be postponed

** This includes independents and numerous regional parties which are often represented in only one of the federal states (e.g. Telugu Desam in Andhra Pradesh etc.)

Table 2: Percentages of the National Vote, 1984-1998

Year	Congress	BJP	JP	Congress +BJP+JP	CPI	CPM	Others
1984	48.0	7.4	6.7	62.1	2.7	5.7	29.5
1989	39.5	11.5	17.7	68.7	2.6	6.5	22.2
1991	36.6	20.0	10.8	67.4	2.5	6.1	24.0
1996	28.8	20.3	8.1	57.2	2.0	6.1	30.7
1998	26.4	26.0	3.3	55.7	1.8	5.3	37.2

It is well known that the prevailing election system usually rewards the winner with a higher percentage of seats than what would be due to him if the distribution of seats would follow a strictly proportional system. The options in this game are either a massive national presence, contesting all seats, or a strategic concentration on strongholds. Electoral alliances can also help in this respect. A comparison of the number of seats presented in Table 1 with the percentage of the vote listed in Table 2 shows the benefit derived from electoral alliances very clearly. Congress and the BJP gained about the same percentage of the national vote in 1998, but the BJP won 38 more seats than the Congress. The electoral alliances of the BJP with several regional parties obviously contributed to this success. In 1989 the JP had profited from electoral alliances in a similar way. While it got only 17.7 per cent of the national vote it won 26.8 per cent of the seats. The other road to success, the massive national presence, was demonstrated for the last time by the Congress in 1984 when it gained 48 per cent of the vote but won 78.6 per cent of the seats.

The smaller parties listed under "Others" have been underrepresented in all the five elections mentioned above. For them the relation between the percentage of the vote gained and that of the seats won has been as follows: 1984 29.5/13.5 , 1989 22.2/11.1, 1991 24/11.7, 1996 30,7/28.8, 1998 37,2/33.8. The underrepresentation was massive from 1984 to 1991 and rather slight in 1996 and 1998. If one only looks at the number of seats won by "Others" one tends to view their emergence as an extraordinary phenomenon of the recent elections. But an analysis of the votes gained by "Others" indicates that they have always attracted a considerable percentage of the national vote. It would be interesting to find out in detail to what extent the electoral alliances of the BJP with regional parties has helped them to "surface", i.e. to convert their share of the vote into a commensurate share of the seats. In order to remove the Congress from its pedestal as the dominant national party, the BJP had to mount a two-pronged attack: challenge the Congress directly in constituencies where this was possible and help "Others" to dislodge the Congress where the BJP was not yet strong enough. This has worked well, though at the cost that "Others" have also come into the limelight.

The new trend of political development established by the distribution of seats after the 1996 election would indicate a rise of federal coalitions based on regional parties and a reduced role of national parties such as Congress, BJP and JP. Whereas these three national parties had won about 80 per cent of all seats in 1984, 1988 and 1991, their share dropped to 63 per cent in 1996. The decline of the Congress party which still remained the most important party in terms of its nationwide spread was particularly ominous in this respect. The JP lost its national stature and was reduced to a regional party, having strongholds only in Bihar and Karnataka. The BJP had its strongholds in five North Indian states and could not yet claim to be a truly national party. The 1998 elections further accentuated the trend towards regionalisation. The JP broke up into several state units which contested the elections under new names. One of them is the Rashtriya Janata Dal in Bihar, another the Lok Shakti of Karnataka. The BJP extended its nationwide spread beyond its five Northern strongholds, particularly by winning 13 seats in Karnataka and getting 3 seats in Tamilnadu. But in general terms the verdict of the electorate was as uncertain in 1998 as it had been in 1996. Moreover, the share of the seats of the parties listed under "Others" increased from 29 per cent in 1996 to 34 per cent in 1998. There were 34 parties in this category, 11 of which captured only one seat each. The number of seats contested by such small parties was also very limited. Only the biggest of them, the Samajwadi Party contested 163 seats and won 20 of them.

Table 3 showing the state-wise election returns of 1998 for all parties which gained at least 12 seats illustrates the trend towards regionalisation even more strikingly. The CPM, with 32 seats third in rank among Indian parties, is of importance only in West Bengal and Kerala, the Samajwadi Party, fourth in rank, is restricted to Uttar Pradesh, the ADMK, fifth in rank, is by definition a Tamil party, the RJD, sixth in rank, has its only stronghold in Bihar and so does the SAP, seventh in rank which holds 10 seats there and only two additional ones in neighbouring Uttar Pradesh. Finally the TDP, eighth in rank, is by definition restricted to Andhra Pradesh.

In some states the 1998 elections led to surprising results which completely upset earlier political calculations. One of these surprises was the Congress comeback in Maharashtra where the BJP in coalition with a local party, the Shiv Sena, was in charge of the state government. Sharad Pawar, the Congress leader and Ex-Chief Minister of Maharashtra thus promptly emerged as the leader of the Congress party in Parliament. The other surprise was the comeback of the All-India Anna Dravida Munnetra Kazhagam (AIADMK) led by Ex-Chief Minister Jayalalitha in Tamilnadu. In the 1996 elections when both parliamentary elections and state assembly elections were held simultaneously in Tamilnadu, the AIADMK had been wiped out. It had lost all its seats in the Lok Sabha where it used to be an ally of the Congress party, as well as in the state assembly where it was opposed by the regional branch of the Congress party. In fact, this branch had severed its connection with the Indian National Congress and had adopted a new name, Tamil Maanila Congress (TMC), due to its difference with the national leadership concerning Jayalalitha and her party. The TMC had bagged 20 parliamentary seats in 1996 and had thus become a major partner of the United Front government. In 1998 this situation was completely reversed, the TMC retained only 3 seats whereas the AIADMK won 18 seats. Jayalalitha had concluded an electoral alliance with the BJP which, as was mentioned before, won 3 seats in Tamilnadu. Nevertheless, after her spectacular success Jayalalitha behaved as if she could act as a kingmaker on the national scene by either supporting or forestalling a BJP-led government at the centre.

Table 3: Number of parliamentary seats held by 8 major parties* in 17 Indian states** (1998)

	BJP	Cong.	CPM	SP	ADMK	RJD	SAP	TDP
Andhra P.	4	22	–	–	–	–	–	12
Assam	1	10	–	–	–	–	–	–
Bihar	19	5	–	–	–	17	10	–
Delhi	6	1	–	–	–	–	–	–
Gujarat	19	7	–	–	–	–	–	–
Haryana	1	3	–	–	–	–	–	–
Himachal P.	2	1	–	–	–	–	–	–
Karnataka	13	9	–	–	–	–	–	–
Kashmir	1	1	–	–	–	–	–	–
Kerala	–	8	6	–	–	–	–	–
Madhya P.	30	10	–	–	–	–	–	–
Maharashtra	4	33	–	–	–	–	–	–
Orissa	7	5	–	–	–	–	–	–
Panjab	3	–	–	–	–	–	–	–
Rajasthan	5	–	–	–	–	–	–	–
Tamilnadu	3	–	–	–	18	–	–	–
Uttar P.	57	–	–	20	–	–	2	–
W. Bengal	1	1	24	–	–	–	–	–
Total (17 states)	176	121	30	20	18	17	12	12
Total India	**179**	**141**	**32**	**20**	**18**	**17**	**12**	**12**

* The 8 major parties are those which have captured 12 seats or more: Bharatiya Jananta Party, Congress, Communist Party (Marxist), Samajwadi Party, All-India Anna Dravida Munnetra Khazagam, Rashtriya Janata Dal, Samata Party, Telugu Desam Party.

** The list of states excludes smaller states such as Goa, Mizoram, Nagaland etc., and Union Territories under the administration of the central government.

A third important regional factor in the national equation was the Telugu Desam Party (TD) of Andhra Pradesh. It had won 16 out of 42 parliamentary seats in its state in 1996 and its leader, Chandrababu Naidu, heads the state government. He had been the convener of the United Front and had thus played a decisive role in national politics. In 1998 the TD captured 12 seats. With the United Front defeated and state elections to be faced in the future, Naidu was between the devil and the deep sea when it came to make his choice at the national level. Both national parties were bound to challenge him at the state elections. He therefore announced that he would adopt a policy of equidistance between the Congress and the BJP and that he would vote neither for nor against the BJP if it was invited to form the government at the centre. Eventually the TD-parliamentarians voted for the BJP, but before that happened Naidu, the erstwhile kingmaker, had a hard time in performing his equidistant exercises.

The Composition of the New Government

Keeping the verdict of the electorate in mind, one can imagine how difficult it was to form a government under such adverse conditions. Moreover, the President had learned a lesson from his predecessor's predicament in 1996. At that time the President had simply invited A.B. Vajpayee as leader of the largest party to try his hand at forming a government. After being sworn in as Prime Minister, Vajpayee had resigned even before facing the vote in the House, because he could not find enough coalition partners. This time the President demanded documentary proof of the required support (272 members) in advance. The BJP had concluded electoral pacts with a series of small parties. Now Vajpayee had to see to it that they would give him letters of support. He had to line up at least 93 parliamentarians in addition to the 179 of his own party. When he had to report to the President on March 12 he could only assure him of the support of 240 members. Jayalalitha had not yet sent in her letter of support and had made the most of keeping Vajpayee on tenterhooks. She made all kinds of statements, once indicating that she would not mind participating in the government, then again promising outside support only. She had also staked high claims for ministerial positions as well as asking for the dismissal of the Tamilnadu government run by her rivals. Finally she climbed down and was satisfied with 2 positions in the cabinet and 2 ministers of state. But there was no doubt left that this government would be at her mercy. Of course, she would not want to forgo a share of power at the centre because she has to defend her position in Tamilnadu where her rivals would be only too eager to prosecute her on charges of corruption.

Vajpayee's other allies were less troublesome than Jayalalitha, but they also had to be accommodated. George Fernandes, leader of the small socialist Samata Party which had won 12 seats became defence minister. Ramkrishna Hegde of the Lok Shakti which had won 3 seats was appointed Commerce Minister. He had once been Chief Minister of Karnataka for the Janata Party and had subsequently been sidelined by H.D. Deve Gowda who became Prime Minister of the United Front government. Hegde then broke away from the JP and established his own little party. But as a prominent politician who had opted for supporting the BJP, he could not be neglected. Another new ally of the BJP is the Trinamul Congress of West Bengal led by the firebrand Mamata Banerji. She had all along been a fiercely anti-communist Congress leader in her state. When she fell out with the Congress leadership she founded her own party and befriended the BJP. "Trinamul" stands for "grassroots" and denotes that this party is supposed to be closer to the people than the old Congress. Only 7 members represent this party in the Lok Sabha. It did not join the government and opted for outside support. The Shiromani Akali Dal with 8 seats sent S.S. Barnala into the cabinet who had once been Chief Minister of the Panjab. The ambitious Shiv Sena of Maharashtra which had contested 79 and won 6 seats was also given a berth in the cabinet. There are also three prominent independents among the ministers: the pugnacious Bombay lawyer Ram Jethmalani and the Ex-Congress Minister Buta Singh in the cabinet and Maneka Gandhi, the widow of Sanjay Gandhi, as a minister of state.

Having to accommodate so many allies the BJP had to be satisfied with 10 of the 21 posts in the cabinet and 14 of the 21 posts of ministers of state. The "classical" ministries, Home, Finance and External Affairs, were kept firmly in the hands of the BJP. Lal Advani, the BJP-President and the real power behind the throne, opted for the Home Ministry which gives him control over the police. He will thus be the guardian of law and order. For the Finance Ministry the BJP selected an ex-civil servant, Yaswant Sinha, who had briefly served as a minister in the minority government of Prime Minister Chandrashekhar (1990/91). The Ministry of Human Resources Development, the erstwhile education ministry, is headed by M.M. Joshi as cabinet minister and Uma Bharati as minister of state. This indicates that the BJP is eager to make a mark in national education as both these ministers are known to be BJP-hardliners. The same is true of Sushma Swaraj who is the cabinet minister of Information and Broadcasting thus controlling the media, a field which the BJP wishes to dominate. Vajpayee combines the position of External Affairs Minister with that of the Prime Minister.

While the formation of the government revealed no unexpected features and was characterised by a restraint of the BJP in claiming ministerial positions, the new government soon surprised the nation by a totally unprecedented move: all governors were asked to resign and most of them were immediately replaced by BJP-men. The governors are appointed by the central government and thus this action was within the four corners of constitutional law, but it certainly deviated from established conventions. Of course, the BJP had been provoked by an equally "unconventional" move of the Governor of Uttar Pradesh, Romesh Bhandari, who had toppled the

BJP-government of this state in the midst of the election campaign, swearing in a new chief minister who had served as a minister in that government but then claimed that he was supported by a majority of the assembly. This farce was soon terminated by a judicial verdict and the governor should have been dismissed. The President wished to do this, but he needed the consent of the central government which dragged its feet because one of the cabinet ministers was involved in this coup. That the new government would wish to dismiss this particular governor was understandable, but dismissing all of them seemed to be an "overkill". The hidden agenda behind it may be that the new governors could be helpful in toppling state governments headed by the rivals of the BJP. From the discussion of the composition of the central government we know that it contains several ministers who would gladly support the dismissal of the government of their home state.

When asked about the criteria for selecting the new governors a senior party member of the BJP admitted that the appointments had been made "keeping in view the dedicated service of the persons to the party". Some of the new governors are ex-civil servants or retired army officers, but even some of those have previous links with the BJP. In one conspicuous case the incumbent was retained: P.C. Alexander continued to be Governor of Maharashtra, because the state government consisting of a coalition of the BJP with the Shiv Sena had recommended this. Uttar Pradesh, India's most populous state, was entrusted to Suraj Bhan, the former deputy speaker of the Lok Sabha. A senior BJP-leader, Sundar Singh Bhandari, was sent to Bihar, a state in which a change of government may be imminent.

Internal Affairs and Indian Federalism

The real test of the BJP-led government will come in the field of internal affairs and it is for good reasons that Lal Advani has seen to it that he is in charge of the Home

Ministry. He is an experienced agitator and he knows how to bring down a government, now he has to show that he also knows how to keep a government in power. Given the tenuous base of this power this means making compromises and postponing the implementation of some points which have been high on the BJP-agenda. One of these points is the introduction of a uniform civil code which would also apply to Indian Muslims who have so far been permitted to follow their own Islamic injunctions concerning matters of marriage and divorce, inheritance etc. The Hindu law had been reformed by Jawaharlal Nehru, but he had not dared to touch Muslim law so as not to offend the Muslim community. In this way he had also secured the Muslim vote for the Indian National Congress. This policy has been defended in the name of secularism, but the BJP has criticised this as pseudo-secularism.

Under the prevailing election system the Indian Muslims have no chance if they would wish to rely on a Muslim party which would never be able to get a seat in the Lok Sabha. With the exception of Kashmir the Muslims are a diaspora community in India. However, with about 11 per cent of the total population they constitute an important vote bank. The Congress used to profit from befriending them earlier, but they then shifted their support to the JP and latterly to the Samajwadi Party, but certainly not to the BJP. The BJP claims some Muslim support and has even appointed a Muslim cabinet minister, Sikander Bakht, but according to election surveys only about 7 per cent of the Muslims voted for the BJP. It is highly unlikely that the BJP will go ahead with the imposition of a uniform civil code under the present conditions. But it is difficult to make any predictions here. Feeling strong after "going nuclear", the BJP may well go ahead with this point of its party programme, too.

Another crucial problem is the support of the Dalits (Untouchables) and the so-called Other Backward Castes (OBC). They have earlier been in the Congress fold. The President of India, K.R. Narayanan, who used to be a

Congress minister, is the first Dalit to occupy this high office. The OBC is a new category which came into the limelight when V.P. Singh resurrected the recommendations of the Mandal Commission Report which had promised reservations of government posts also to such castes which are not Dalits but feel themselves equally suppressed by the upper castes. This was a special problem of Northern India because in Southern India the OBC had long since captured political power. V.P. Singh had thought of favouring the OBC as a move to check the advance of the BJP. Actually he himself had helped the BJP to increase its strength by the electoral pact of 1989, but then he had turned around and had pitted the OBC against the upper caste BJP. In 1990 several young men of the upper castes had immolated themselves as the positions open to them in government service were dwindling due to OBC-reservations. The BJP was quick to cash in on this upsurge against V.P. Singh's policy, but it was careful not to attack the OBC and rather played the Hindu card, stressing national solidarity. After all, the BJP was also having an eye on the OBC-electorate and did not wish to get stuck with the image of an upper caste party. As the election results have shown, the BJP has been quite successful in following this line. In this way it has also been able to make inroads into the South were the upper castes are a small minority and the OBC are very numerous. Election surveys have shown that the BJP has attracted a considerable portion of the OBC vote in 1998 whereas the Dalits have mostly voted for the Congress party. The policy of the BJP-led government will be aimed at coopting OBC and Dalits even at the risk of alienating its original upper caste clientele. The upper castes have nobody else to turn to but the BJP and therefore their support can be taken for granted.

The BJP also has to come to terms with Indian federalism by trying to capture power in more federal states and by forgetting about its earlier centralism. The precursor of the BJP, the Bharatiya Jan Sangh, wanted to abolish federalism altogether and establish India as a unitary state. It also wanted to go ahead with Hindi as a national language. Actually Hindi is the national language according to the constitution, but its imposition has been resented by the South. Therefore all central governments have been going slow on this and the BJP-led government will have to do the same, the more so as it has just begun to get a foothold in the South. Indian federalism still shows the traces of its colonial origin. The British introduced it in 1935 by granting "provincial autonomy" while at the same time keeping imperial control firmly in the hands of the Viceroy and his council. The Viceroy could also suspend "provincial autonomy" in one or more provinces and this has become "President's Rule" in independent India. Critics have long since argued that this is incompatible with genuine federalism. But central governments have all along been very reluctant to relinquish this powerful instrument. The United Front government which was in fact a federal coalition could have been expected to abolish "President's Rule", but it failed to do so. Its precarious position did not permit such a bold measure. The BJP will certainly not abandon this instrument and it will be interesting to watch which state will be the first target of its application under the new dispensation.

Another important aspect of Indian federalism is the distribution of financial resources. The scheme of allocating taxes to the centre and the provinces under British rule was designed so as to leave static taxes such as the land revenue to the provinces while keeping dynamic ones like income tax and customs in central hands. The income tax was finally shared 50/50 between the centre and the states, but customs remained a central revenue. Independent India adopted this imperial heritage. As long as India followed a protectionist regime, import duties were not a great source of revenue income, but when external trade was liberalised under Rajiv Gandhi, the income from import duties soon dwarfed all other income of the central government. Looking at the increasing income of the centre the federal states clamoured for a greater share of the growing cake, but they did not get it. The only way of getting more was by overspending and then waiting for the centre to bail them out. This is, of course, no healthy approach to federal finance. Again, the United Front government could have been expected to change the ground rules and to put federal finance on a sound foundation, but it did not do anything about it before it was unceremoniously scuttled. The BJP with its original centralist bias can hardly be expected to become federalist now. It will therefore stick to the existing arrangements and defend them in the name of national unity.

The Conduct of Indian Foreign Policy

India's foreign policy had so far been characterised by a high degree of continuity. Changes at the helm of external affairs had never meant a new departure in policy making. This was also true of Vajpayee's term of office (1977-1979). He was at that time a pioneer in trying to normalise relations with China and was snubbed by Deng Xiaoping who started a war against Vietnam when Vajpayee visited China and then even compared that war to the one which China had waged against India in 1962. Presumably Vajapayee has not forgotten this experience, but this does not mean that he would now adopt a vindictive stance towards China. However, he did not contradict his Defence Minister, George Fernandes, who said that China constitutes a bigger threat to India than Pakistan. Interpreted with the benefit of hindsight, this statement was obviously meant to prepare the ground for India's nuclear tests, whereas at the time when it was made it appeared to be an uncontrolled outburst characteristic of Fernandes' temper.

Before the BJP came to power it used to state that India would go nuclear once the BJP was able to decide this matter. Apprehensive observers were pleased with a statement on this issue which the Prime Minister made after assuming office. He only repeated the assertion that India should keep its nuclear option open and thus endorsed what his predecessors had said earlier. It seemed that the BJP in office would realise that it is better to maintain the policy of "nuclear ambiguity" than to face the costs of actually going nuclear. These costs can be specified in economic terms as a deployment of nuclear warheads and the maintenance of a delivery system would burden the Indian budget enormously. Moreover, there was the diplomatic cost of isolation. An economic and diplomatic cost/benefit-analysis would certainly show that "going nuclear" does not pay. It seems that the preparations for the recent tests were made in 1995 under the Congress government. A contingency plan produced at that time is supposed to have stated that the decision of going nuclear would delay India's economic progress by five to ten years. Probably the preparations made in 1995 were supposed to enable India to go nuclear if and when Pakistan would conduct such tests. The economic crisis faced by Pakistan in recent months did not seem to permit such tests. Therefore nobody expected India's five underground nuclear blasts of May 11 and 13, 1998 which even included a hydrogen bomb. Unlike in 1974 when a single blast at the same site in the Rajasthan desert was termed as that of a "nuclear device" as a test for the peaceful use of atomic energy, the present blasts were openly referred to as tests of atomic bombs with a view to ascertain their use for different types of weapons. Vajpayjee in making this announcement congratulated the Indian scientists who had conducted these tests. If the tests had been conducted a as reaction to a Pakistani test, such an announcement would have been understandable. But now the BJP took on the responsibility of acting as a pace-setter in this field, forcing Pakistan to take up this challenge. Those Indians who had voted for the BJP in full knowledge of its nuclear programme obviously felt elated by the blasts. Observers who still see India as a nation that claims Mahatma Gandhi to be its "Father" can only feel sad at this turn of events. Gandhi once referred to the atombomb as "the violence of the cowards" but the leaders of the BJP probably think of themselves as brave champions of India's national honour. The new political regime has dropped its "convenient mask" although Vajpayee still heads the government.

The major touchstone of Indian foreign policy is, of course, the relationship with Pakistan. In this respect, a BJP-led government seemed to have an advantage. Some Pakistani policy makers have said that they would rather deal with a BJP-government than with any other Indian government. Whether they still think so after the nuclear blasts remains to be seen. Stymied by the threat of American sanctions which would precipitate Pakistan's bankruptcy, its leaders at first seemed to hesitate to go nuclear immediately. But the pressure to match India's performance and to achieve parity with India in this way were obviously greater than any considerations of financial prudence. India's brinkmanship was perhaps not aimed at letting Pakistan go bankrupt in this way, because India could not be interested in having a bankrupt neighbour. But whatever India's leader may have thought when going nuclear, they obviously did not worry about the stability of the region. Some Western security analysts now envisage a scenario of open mutual deterrence between India and Pakistan like that which prevailed between the two superpowers during the Cold War. The Cold War was not a cosy affair and became finally an economic war of attrition which ended with the bankruptcy and disintegration of the Soviet Union. It is therefore not exactly an attractive model for the future relations between India and Pakistan. Moreover, some of the elements which prevented a nuclear escalation of the Cold War such as Europe as an intervening factor and the long distance separating the superpowers from each other do no exist as far as India and Pakistan are concerned. They are next-door neighbours and any "misguided" missile may trigger off a nuclear holocaust. The fall-out of the coming to power of a new political regime in India cannot yet be fully examined. The prospects for regional stability are dim unless both India and Pakistan now sign the NPT and CTBT after having demonstrated their nuclear credentials.

But the economic "fall-out" will not be easily controlled.

India's friendship with Russia will probaby not be affected by the change of government in India. Even in the days of the Soviet Union this friendship was not based on any ideological affinities but on national interest. There is no reason that this relationship will no longer be perceived in this way by both partners. The nuclear blasts have been criticised by President Yeltsin, who felt that India had let him down. But he will not do anything about it, the more so as he faces urgent problems at home. The relations between India and the USA have always been problematic. American policymakers never had an abiding interest in South Asia and looked at the subcontinent from the point of view of their immediate security concerns. Thus they would support a "front state" Pakistan whenever that was convenient and forget about South Asia when they were busy elsewhere. American security perceptions are also swayed by fashions. John Foster Dulles pontificated at an early stage that the Hindus of India may be taken in by the Communists. Islam was then seen as a bulwark against Communism. In recent years the scare of Islamic fundamentalism has made the American look for allies in other places. Samuel Huntingdon's "Clash of Civilisations" is a recent case in point. Seen in this light, Hindu nationalism may now qualify for special American attention in a quest to combat Islamic fundamentalism. This would be an extremely dangerous tendency and it is to be hoped that no Indian government will be impressed by this new American fashion. At present there is anyhow no prospect of a special Indo-American friendship.The American reaction against the nuclear blasts was predictable. President Clinton was obliged by law to impose sanctions. The Indian government must have been aware of this and obviously did not mind snubbing the United States. The unfortunate consequences of this confrontation will be felt in the economic field. But since India is not yet as much integrated into the world economy as the advocates of liberalisation had wanted it to be, American sanctions will not hurt India very much, but they would encourage all those who harp on "self-reliance". Thus India's reaction to American sanctions may be more important than the sanctions themselves.

The Economy: "Swadeshi" versus Liberalisation

In the days when the Congress was wedded to socialism, the BJP projected itself as a protagonist of liberalisation. When the Congress adopted liberalisation as its new economic creed it stole the thunder of the BJP and made it look for other ways and means of regaining an economic profile. Actually some Indian industrialists who are afraid of increasing international competition would be allies of the BJP if it advocated a more cautious economic policy. Indian industry had after all grown up in a period of protectionism favouring import substitution and breeding export-pessimism. The chances of exporting quality products were small with this background whereas the danger of losing out to imports of foreign goods was looming larger as liberalisation progressed. The venerable term "swadeshi" was resurrected in this context. In the days of the freedom movement this had been the message of those who wished to get along without British goods replacing them with those made in India (swa=own, desh=country).Due to this heritage, the term "swadeshi" has an emotional political content and reflects much more than mere economic calculations.

Even before the elections of 1996 the Congress politicians had lost the courage of their convictions and had eliminated the word "liberalisation" from their vocabulary. They merely referred to "economic reforms" which sounded somewhat non-commital. This did not help them in scoring points in the election. On the contrary, it put them on the defensive. In this political atmosphere the BJP could not be expected to reclaim their earlier initative in advocating liberalisation. An emphasis on "swadeshi" was more attractive. This did not mean that anybody wanted to abolish the reforms introduced so far. But the momentum was lost . The pace set in the years from 1991 to 1993 was not kept up. The political instability ushered in by the elections of 1996 contributed to a further slowdown of the urge for reforms and finally also to a reduction of economic growth. The recent nuclear blasts will further restrict the momentum of economic reforms, their negative "fall-out" will actually provide a good excuse for the government, because sanctions imposed by foreign powers can then be blamed for anything that goes wrong with the Indian economy. The first BJP-budget presented on June 1, 1998 showed no attempt at attracting foreign capital in order to balance the negative effect of economic sanctions. The Finance Minister stated that he did not expect any impact of such sanctions but nevertheless earmarked Rs. 57 billion in the budget as a contingency fund to be drawn upon if the sanctions do come into effect. He also raised the amount allocated for defence expenditure by 14 per cent and indicated that he may have to provide even more funds for this purpose. All commentators spoke of a "swadeshi"-budget. In view of the emphasis on defence expenditure one may even call it a defiant budget which conveys a message to the world that India could not care less about credit ratings and other expressions of international disapproval of its policy.

India's slowdown in recent years has prevented it from getting involved in the Asian crisis. The Indian elephant lumbered on while the Asian tigers licked their wounds. The Asian crisis was not caused by the profligacy of governments but rather by the carelessness of foreign investors and Asian businessmen who spent borrowed money recklessly as long as the going was good. The avalanche of devaluations precipitated by the advice of the IMF then made matters worse. Actually the IMF which acts as a firebrigade on behalf of international creditors shot itself in the foot by giving this advice, because devaluation increased the burden of debt and this required a massive bailout which stretched the resources of the IMF to the limit. The fact that India was not yet institutionally prepared for absorbing foreign investment in the same way as the Asian tigers shielded it from the impact of the crisis. Moreover, India's export earnings from goods produced at low wages are not yet of such dimensions that a competitive devaluation would be required so as to face the challenge of the exports of the Asian tigers. And last but not least devaluation would make imports more expensive. This may be helpful if the import bill includes many items which are not of immediate need for the economy, but India's major imports are petroleum and investment goods. This means that the import bill could only be curtailed by sacrificing economic growth. The new government would probably just hold the line and refrain from making major changes in economic and monetary policy.Whether liberalisation could be encouraged once more after the current problems have been overcome depends on many conditions which cannot be discussed here in detail. One point which may be stressed here is that previous governments have conceived of liberalisation mainly in terms of macro-economic reforms. India now needs institutional reforms in many different fields. It has to be seen whether the new government can make headway in this respect.

Future Perspectives

As mentioned in the beginning, India has witnessed the rise of a new regime, and the recent nuclear blasts have shown, that inspite of the uncertain verdict of the electorate and the precarious nature of coalition politics, the party in power will do whatever it thinks fit. We may now try to speculate what kind of future courses of development may be in store for India. One scenario would be that of a collapse of the government due to its precarious support by allies whose loyalties cannot be taken for granted. For the time being these allies are kept in line, because they have no other option. The Congress is not in a position to attract these allies at present. Of course, an ally – particulary a regional party – may withdraw when it feels that it does not need the support of the BJP any longer for settling its scores. If Jayalalitha, for instance, sweeps the assembly elections in Tamilnadu and re-emerges as a powerful chief minister she would be able to drive another hard bargain, eventually even toppling the central government and looking for partners elsewhere.

Another scenario would be that of the survival of the BJP-led government for the full length of its term. If the electorate then feels that the BJP has done well it may give it a better mandate, but it may also turn against the government due to the pendulum-effect which has characterised many elections in India. In this case the Congress may stage a comeback, but this depends on its ability to renew its vigour while spending a full term in the opposition. The BJP may feel tempted to preempt such a Congress-comeback by precipitating an early election at a time when it feels strong. But the Indian people may resent another premature election and thus the Congress may get enough time to put its house in order.The Congress has been beset with many ailments in recent years, one of them has been a lack of leadership. Moreover, the Congress would have to beat the BJP at the game of wooing allies. Coalition politics has come to stay and the Congress would have to stoop to conquer if it wishes to come to power once more. If the small parties which are at present coalition partners of the BJP feel that they are going to be absorbed by the major partner they may opt for a Congress-led coalition to save their skin. Of course, some of them may actually merge with the BJP if their leaders think that this will help them to remain in power. The political situation with regard to these small parties is extremely fluid and predictions of their behaviour are very difficult.

If the present trend towards regionalisation as exemplified by the increase in the category "Others" to about one third of the parliamentary seats continues, there may emerge a scenario in which the two national parties – the Congress and the BJP – will occupy only one half of the parliamentary seats while the other half is filled by highly fragmented "Others". In fact, in terms of the percentages of the national vote those two parties even at present account only for 52 per cent. If they are cut down to size, i.e. their number of seats would be more or less equal to the percentage of the vote gained, a new situation could arise. The Congress has already been cut down to size in the 1998 election, this could very well happen to the BJP in future elections. Coalition-building would then require great skill and small parties could drive hard bargains. A new generation of politicians may be better equipped to deal with such problems than those who are used to the old style of politics. However, the tasks of the future, especially economic development based on institutional reforms, would require not necessarily a strong but a stable government. Economic prosperity and the alleviation of mass poverty does not require constant bureaucratic intervention but clear guidelines and predictable action both by government and the private sector. India's human resources are of enormous dimensions both in quantity and quality. The future would be bright, if they could be used well.

References:

Jaffrelot, Christophe (1996), *The Hindu Nationalist Movement and Indian Politics, 1925 to the 1990s*, London

Kulke, Hermann and Dietmar Rothermund (1997), *A History of India*, London (Third Revised ed.)

Dietmar Rothermund (ed.) (1996), *Liberalising India. Progress and Problems*, New Delhi

7

NATIONALISM AND THE RECONSTRUCTION OF TRADITIONS IN ASIA

The Quest for a Useful Past in the Interest of National Solidarity

Nationalism has been imported into Asia from the West, but for this very reason it had to be defended by linking it to indigenous traditions. The time-lag between the rise of nationalism in the West and its appearance in Asia was relatively short, in most cases less than a hundred years. The phenomenon of reconstructed traditions could be observed both in the West and in the Non-Western world. Only the methods of such reconstruction were perhaps somewhat more self-conscious and deliberate in the Non-Western world. In characterising such deliberate methods one speaks nowadays of the "invention of tradition". In its paradoxical meaning this term captures the quest for a tradition which suits the ideological programme of those who look for a useful past in order to justify their present needs. But the term is misleading because it suggests a complete freedom of choice in making up whatever "tradition" one may find useful. In this way the historical conditions which limit this freedom of choice are not taken into account. It seems to be more appropriate to speak of a "reconstruction of tradition". This implies that there are elements of tradition actually available which are re-interpreted so as to suit the purpose of ideologues. Such elements are necessarily specific to the respective cultural context. Nevertheless there is a common agenda of those who reconstruct traditions of this kind: they are pursuing a quest for national solidarity. The usefulness of traditions is judged in terms of their contribution to such a solidarity. If actual traditions are rooted in divisive social organisations like caste, clan and tribe etc. they tend to be ignored. At the most they are referred to in an apologetic manner or invested with a new meaning so as to fit in with "solidarity traditionalism". (Rothermund 1979)

Accordingly we can see in Asia a fascinating panorama of reconstructed traditions which reflect the varied cultural heritage as well as the common need for constituting and maintaining the nation state which in its modern form was certainly not an element of this heritage. The nation state is the dominating political form of our times. It implies a well-defined territory, a more or less homogenous population and some kind of representative government. In fact, ever since the sovereignty of the people rather than that of rulers has become the universal principle of state formation, it was necessary to determine "national" boundaries delineating the constituency on which this new type of sovereignty ought to be based. In theory the sovereignty of the people could encompass all of mankind, but in practice it has been restricted to more manageable proportions. The way in which such manageable proportions have been arrived at has always been the outcome of a chequered history. But once the "nation state" was formed, its history was often interpreted as "manifest destiny".

Many scholars have pointed out that nationalism lacks a theory such as that provided by Liberalism or Marxism. This is due to its hybrid nature as described above. While concepts such as the sovereignty of the people or self-determination may lend themselves to theoretical analysis, the pragmatic determination of the nation state as a unit which embodies these concepts can only be explained historically. This is why nationalism has had a special affinity with history as a discipline. It would be interesting to trace this affinity more in detail, but this would go beyond the scope of this article. Similarly it would exceed our terms of reference to discuss the evolution of the nation state and of nationalism in the West. We may only mention the case of Poland, which is of general interest as it disproves most current theories of the rise of nationalism. According to the British historian, Lord Acton, Poland was the cradle of modern European nationalism due to the very fact that a nation state was denied to the Poles by several divisions of their territory by more powerful rulers in their neighbourhood. Poland shows that nationalism can be particularly virulent if its claims are denied and this is also true of those areas of Asia which were subjected to colonialism. Scholars have opted for various causes of the rise of nationalism such as the impact of the Protestant reformation or the bourgeois and industrial revolutions, but all of these were absent in Poland where the national movement was spearheaded by the nobility at a time when the Polish bourgeoisie was not yet of any importance and industrialisation had still to wait for many decades.. Acton, himself a Catholic nobleman, was more perceptive in assessing the historical importance of Polish nationalism than later writers. His essay "Nationality" was first published in 1862, but has obviously been completely forgotten by modern analysts of nationalism. (Dalberg-Acton 1862)

Before tracing the fate of nationalism and of the traditions reconstructed on its behalf in different Asian countries, we should discuss the motives of nationalists in general. Liberal as well as Marxist thinkers tend to look at nationalism as an instance of "false consciousness", a delusion often propagated by certain interests due to ulterior motives such as power and profit. Unmasking such interests would eradicate nationalism and help people to live by more rational standards. This exorcism of nationalism by means of rationalism neglects the human desire for commitment to a cause. It is this desire which we should take into consideration somewhat more in detail.

The Concept of Rational Choice and the Desire for Commitment to a Cause

The modern social sciences are wedded to the concept of rationality. Only rational decisions can be properly analysed. They are, at least in a probabilistic sense, predictable. The concept of rational choice is based on these assumptions. Choice must be attributed to individuals. But the individualism implied in this way is an atomistic and mechanical one. For instance, in discussing the "prisoner's dilemma", one of the most famous paradigms of the theory of rational choice, we are not interested in the individual qualities of the respective prisoners, but in the fact that they have to arrive at their decisions individually and that they cannot avoid making these decisions. It is difficult to make the transition from this focus on individual rational choice to collective action. Max Weber had tried to cope with this problem in terms of consensus or agreement which may be based on past experiences under similar circumstances. But in general social scientists as well a economists are bound to concentrate on the abstract individual and his/her rational choice. Everything which does not fit into this scheme will be termed irrational and may at best be described in a historical narrative.

This method does not help in understanding the universal human desire for a commitment to one cause or the other. One commitment of this kind is that to one's nation. As Ernest Gellner would argue, this commitment is not a necessary one. (Gellner 1994) There may be other options. Jürgen Habermas has coined the term "constitutional patriotism" to indicate a rational approach to the commitment to a political entity to which one happens to belong. This kind of patriotism would also apply to persons who have acquired a certain nationality whereas they belong to a different one by birth. However, in raising the point concerning the desire for commitment to a cause, we do not wish to refer to such"rational" attitudes, but to the type of commitment which motivates a person to go to jail or to sacrifice his life for the respective cause. Innumerable people who participated in freedom movements in Asia and elsewhere were committed in this way. Their decisions were obviously not determined by rational choice. Trying to explain their behaviour by stating that they obviously followed an irrational urge would not be helpful. Instead of this we should perhaps state that nationalism is a cause which in a very prominent way fulfills the human desire for a committed life. Doing one's duty beyond the sphere that is determined and controlled by others may be a similar form of commitment though of a much humbler type.

There is no doubt that propaganda plays an important role in making nationalism a favourite option for such a commitment. The desire for such a commitment, just like the propensity to fall in love, is initially open ended. Attractive messages must be transmitted and received to clinch the issue. This leads us to the phenomenon of social communication which will be discussed subsequently. At this stage we only wish to emphasise that a whole spectrum of symbols, verbal messages and narratives, monuments etc. are required to project nationalism so as to appear as a successful candidate for the emotional attachment indicated here. This is where the reconstruction of tradition fits in, because it links the past with the present and the community in general with the particular individual. The desire for commitment to a cause is intimately linked with the individual's quest for being part of a larger context which transcends his/her narrowly circumscribed sphere of life.

Social Communication and "Imagined Communities"

When Karl Deutsch wrote his pioneering book "*Nationalism and Social Communication*"(Deutsch 1966) he was mostly concerned with the media that transmitted the message of nationalism and the frequency of communication that knitted the nation together and made it aware of itself. Books, newspapers and, of course, the national language as a medium of instruction all helped to spread nationalism. The level of mass education was essential in this respect. Scholars dealing with Non-Western countries tended to be disappointed by Deutsch's approach and found that if they applied his categories rigorously to the nations they were studying, there should have been no nationalism in those countries at all. (Rothermund 1982) Widespread illiteracy seemed to be an insurmountable barrier to the type of social communication studied by Deutsch. In recent years this lack of attention to the Non-Western world has been remedied by Benedict Anderson's book "*Imagined Communities. Reflections on the Spread and Origin of Nationalism*". (Anderson 1991) Anderson is also concerned with social communication, because he stresses that beyond face-to-face groups all communities are necessarily "imagined", i.e. perceived due to social communication. It is strange, though, that there is no reference to Deutsch's work in Anderson's book. He otherwise quotes many relevant authors, and it seems improbable that he should have never read Deutsch, who is conspicuous by his absence from his text and his bibliography.

In the third chapter of his book Anderson discusses the origins of national consciousness and dwells mainly on print-capitalism and print-languages thus parallelling Deutsch's research programme. But being aware of the Non-Western world, he states:"... the concrete formation of contemporary nation-states is by no means isomorphic with the determinate reach of particular print-languages". (Anderson 1991: 46) Anderson's comments on the colonial experience are more instructive than his more general reflections on the rise of national consciousness. He mentions that the colonial rulers ordered their Asian subjects to celebrate their national festivals, e.g., the centennial of the national liberation of the Dutch from French imperialism, without taking note of the fact that those subjects might see the analogy between this and their own liberation. He quotes an Indonesian nationalist, Suwardi Surjaningrat (Ki Hadjar Dewantoro), who wrote in 1913: "If I were a Dutchman, I would not organise an independence celebration in a country where the independence of the people has been stolen."(Anderson 1991: 117)

One of the most interesting chapters of Anderson's book is that on"Census, Map, Museum" which he added to the revised edition of his book in 1991. (Anderson 1991: 163-185) Here he deals with elements of social communication which were of special significance for the Asian colonies of European powers. The census created a new type of classification and quantification. Sudipta Kaviraj has called this elsewhere the transition from "fuzzy" to "enumerated identities". (Kaviraj 1992: 39) This gave a new direction to the "imagination" of communities. Similarly the production of maps based on scientific surveys provided a clear picture of the respective territoriality which could then even emerge as a logo of the colony or state. Adapting Kaviraj's terms we could call this a transition from a "fuzzy" to a "delimited territoriality". And finally there was the museum dominated by imperial archaeologists who posed as guardians of the past of the subject people. It may be said that they processed the raw material which helped the nationalists in their reconstruction of a useful past.

At the centre of social communication is undoubtedly the language issue which is beset by many problems. (Hellmann-Rajanayagam and Rothermund 1992) In spite of the fact that national movements in Asia were often directed against the predominance of the languages of their rulers, those languages nevertheless served as a medium of nationalist discourse. First of all they contained the terminology required for this discourse. Furthermore, they provided a *lingua franca* for nationalists from various regions of the respective country who spoke regional languages, as those in other regions would otherwise not understand them. The idea that a nation should also have a national language impressed all nationalists, but they often found it difficult to agree on a common linguistic denominator. Actually the quest for a national language often led to acrimonious disputes, as we shall see in detail later on. Harking back to a traditional language with a great literary heritage had its own problems. Such a language mostly had no modern prose and, even worse, it might embody styles of speech that did not contribute to the solidarity of the speakers but rather articulated differences in status. In multi-ethnic nations the quest for a national language could lead to a division of the past as particularly those language groups that were in a minority felt excluded from the mainstream and tried to reconstruct a useful past of their own. As social communication increased under the auspices of nationalism, tensions would also increase and sometimes lead to violent conflict. If the ethnic divide was also a religious one, or religious communities articulated their differences in ethnic terms, this would further complicate the issue. The quest for national solidarity could thus produce the very opposite: communal strife and hatred. Under such conditions the human desire for commitment to a cause could take a neurotic turn. This, of course, would be grist for the mill of those who considered nationalism in general to be an irrational affliction of a neurotic type.

India: A House Divided

In discussing specific Asian nations we shall first look at India which has a long history of nationalist thought and action, but which also had to suffer from a cruel awakening from the nationalist dream due to a partition along religious lines which nevertheless did not solve the problem that gave rise to it in the first place.

The British conquest of India will not be discussed here in detail, the only fact to be highlighted here is the time differential between the establishment of British rule in Bengâl in the mid-eighteenth century and the last British territorial acquisitions in the North-West in the late nineteenth century. (Rothermund 1965) Furthermore it should be remembered that the British conquest had a differential impact on the two great religious communities, the Hindus and the Muslims. For the most part India was ruled by Muslims when the British took over and thus the Muslims felt that the British has deprived them of their power whereas the Hindus could initially look upon the British as their liberators from Muslim rule. This was particularly so in Bengal, which had been dominated by the powerful Nawabs of Bengal. In Maharashtra (Western India), whose Hindu rulers the British had vanquished in the early nineteenth century the feelings towards the British were rather different and in a way proto-nationalist at an early stage. In 1849 a Maharashtrian nationalist wrote that the British should be careful in India lest they would be swept away by a revolution as had happened to them in America. (Rothermund 1965: 26) The British were still rather tolerant of such remarks as they did not take them very seriously. They were only shaken by the "Mutiny" of 1857 when disaffected Indian soldiers trained by the British joined hands with landlords and peasants who had felt the burden of stiff British revenue assessments. This was a "post-pacification revolt" of a type noted also elsewhere after colonial rule had left its mark on the societies concerned. (Stokes 1978) It was not backed by the Western-educated Indian elite, which was as shocked by it as the British were. The restoration of the old order which the rebels had in mind would have had no place for this elite. Therefore the nationalism of this elite remained dormant for some time and emerged only in the last decades of the nineteenth century.

The educated high caste Bengalis, also referred to as *bhadralok* (people from good families) were in the vanguard of Indian nationalism. They were the chief architects of the reconstruction of India's glorious past and drew upon the findings of Western Indologists to justify their claims. If one enlarges Anderson's "Museum" so as to include not only artefacts, but also scholarly literature, one could state that the Bengali intelligentsia fully exploited the resources of this "Museum". The glorious past that they saw in this way, was entirely a Hindu past. The Muslims were seen as a foreign power which ruined the glory of India. Moreover, Bengali writers used the literary device of expressing their criticism of British foreign rule by going back in time and making their heroes fight against the Muslims instead of the British in order to escape censorship. But often it was not quite clear whether they adopted this style only for this reason or whether they actually enjoyed indulging in anti-Muslim tirades. (Roy 1995: 123-125) There was also another reason why they needed the Muslims as a counterfoil. The idea of a glorious Hindu past required a definition of the "Hindu". The easiest way of defining a Hindu was that he was not a Muslim. Originally "Hindu" was a term which referred to the people living near or beyond the river Indus. "Hinduism" as a designation of a religion was an invention of Western scholars. The concept of a Hindu nation was accordingly also a new one and the Bengalis were its most eloquent defenders.

The Bengalis were particularly interested in one aspect of ancient Indian philosophy: the monism of Vedanta. By praising the unity of the soul with god they could by a subtle twist also praise the fusion of the individual with the nation. Talking about the salvation (*moksha*) of the soul, they could also hint at national liberation. Moreover, monism interpreted in this way could also legitimise the role of the elite in speaking and acting for the nation as a whole. (Rothermund 1965: 123-125)The basic message derived from this Vedantic nationalism was that India was a nation and could shake off the shackles of foreign rule by an act of consciousness just as the soul could overcome its dualist illusion and recognise that it was one with god. The most important proponent of the new interpretation of Vedanta was Swami Vivekananda whose appearance at the World Parliament of Religions in Chicago in 1893 made a deep impression not only on his Western audience but also on his Indian compatriots. His success in the West seemed to validate the greatness of the Hindu tradition. In reconstructing this tradition, Vivekananda managed to include the modern idea of socialism in his message. He argued persuasively that in contrast to the individualist West, the Indian tradition had always emphasised social responsibility. Service to the community rather than the profit motive had been the hallmark of Indian ethics. (Rothermund 1970)This kind of ascriptive socialism was very attractive even to later Indian socialists like Jawaharlal Nehru.

In Northern India a more earthy revivalist movement inspired by Swami Dayanand Saraswati based its message on the ancient Vedas rather than on the philosophical

Vedanta. The association of the followers of this new creed was called "Arya Samaj". (Rothermund 1965: 34) Some of them were aware of the organisational advantages of the Christian church and spoke of "our Vedic church" when referring to their association. Dayanand wrote a book entitled "Satyarth Prakash" (The Light of Truth) in which the Vedas were portrayed as the source of all knowledge. He was more absolutist in his claims than most Hindu teachers before him, but his followers cherished this assertion of certitude. National solidarity was an important aim of Dayanand's message. Most of his followers dropped their last names, which usually indicated the caste to which they belonged, so as to eradicate all traces of social divisiveness. They claimed, of course, that this was in keeping with the spirit of the Vedas.

Sanskrit, the sacred language of the Vedas, played an increasingly important role in the reconstruction of India's past. Western Indologists had certified that it was the oldest language of the world. Drawing on its venerable heritage became a national duty. Many Indian authors who wrote in the many regional languages of India made it a point to look to Sanskrit when coining new terms. Thus they gave an air of respectability to their works. Hindi, the *lingua franca* of Northern India which was adopted as the national language was inundated with Sanskrit neologisms in this way. Even the Indian constitution recommends this recourse to Sanskrit for the improvement of Hindi. Urdu, the language preferred by the North Indian Muslims, is actually in its basic structure and vocabulary identical with Hindi, except that it is written in a script derived from Arabic and contains many Arabic and Persian words. In a way Urdu and Hindi form a continuum with a great deal of common ground in the middle and a Sanskritised style at one end and a Persianised one at the other. The more Hindu authors favoured a Sanskritised style, the more the Muslims felt linguistically excluded and insisted on the importance of Urdu as a Muslim language. (Dittmer 1972)

Just as the Sanskritisation of Indian languages, the

Hindu reconstructions of Indian tradition excluded the Muslims either implicitly or even explicitly. Dayanand had made disparaging remarks about Islam in his book. Others did not go so far, but it was obvious that their messages were addressed to Hindus only. Actually the Muslims resented the tolerant inclusiveness of many well meaning Hindus more than open attacks. The Bengali saint, Sri Ramakrishna, had referred to all religions as steps to the same well. This was acceptable to all Hindus who anyhow represented numerous paths (*marga*) to salvation, but it was anathema to Muslims, who believed only in one God and his Prophet and could not admit that god could be reached in any other way. The more the Indian Muslims felt challenged by their Hindu countrymen, the more they turned to an extra-territorial allegiance to the centres and authorities of Islam outside India. Orthodox Islam does not tolerate the concept of nationalism anyhow, its concept of solidarity is that of the *umma* the worldwide community of believers. Accordingly Indian Muslims also had little sympathy with Arab nationalism but clung to the authority of the Kalif who represented the unity of all believers.

Indian nationalism was greatly transformed by Mahatma Gandhi (1869-1948) (Rothermund 1989/1998) who was less interested in a useful past than in a useful present to be determined by the people here and now. He had refined his method of *satyagraha* (holding on to truth) in South Africa. People would bind themselves by a solemn oath and jointly transgress unjust laws imposed upon them by the colonial rulers. He tried to transfer this method to India but was initially at a loss to identify unjust laws which could be suitably transgressed. He therefore concentrated on the more general idea of non-cooperation with the British, which was, however, much more difficult to articulate. He was therefore glad to be able to join hands with the Indian Muslims, who were at that time greatly incensed about the treatment of the Kalif by the British after the end of the First World War. Gandhi thought that he could achieve national solidarity by making common cause with the Muslims in this respect. But this was a grave political mistake, because he encouraged the extra-territorial loyalties of the Indian Muslims and this at a time when the Kalif was soon to be dumped by his own people. M.A. Jinnah, at that time still a liberal constitutionalist among Muslim leaders, had warned Gandhi in vain against taking this step. When the cause was lost, the Muslims forgot about national solidarity and followed a communal course in Indian politics. Jinnah, who felt that he could not make a career in Indian politics as a liberal constitutionalist, opted for this communal course. (Wolpert 1984)

Jinnah was a sober lawyer who was not particularly interested in the reconstruction of tradition in terms of the glory of Islam. But his contemporary, the poet M. Iqbal, was deeply impressed by this past glory. He also admired Nietzsche's philosophy and interpreted the decline of Islam as a loss of the will to power. Iqbal expressed his ideas in moving poetry, but he also participated in practical politics and in his address as president of the Muslim League in 1930, he for the first time demanded the establishment of an autonomous Muslim state in North-Western India. (Wolpert 1984: 123) Jinnah was initially not attracted by this idea as he was the leader of the Muslim diaspora in India. But the course of political events pushed him into the same direction and in his speech as president of the Muslim League in 1940 he propounded his two-nations-theory according to which "Hindus and Muslims are two nations by any definition of the term". He was careful not to reveal the territorial limits of "his" nation, as it then would have become obvious that he had to betray his earlier constituency, the Muslim diaspora which finally had to remain in India.

The attempt at reconstructing a national tradition in India finally led to a division of the past as well as of the present and the future. The increase of social communication had hastened this process. The "constitutional patriotism" advocated by Habermas might have prevented this tragedy. This was also the kind of secular nationalism represented by Jawaharlal Nehru who did go to jail and demonstrated that it was not necessary to appeal to religious or quasi-religious traditions in order to mobilise people for the national cause. But the masses were more readily mobilised by Gandhi whose symbols and metaphors referred to the Hindu tradition. He also referred to Allah in his prayers, but to an orthodox Muslim such references by a non-believer were an insult rather than an invitation to national solidarity.

The Tragedy of Sri Lanka

The history of Sri Lanka provides another example of communal strife which could not be overcome by national solidarity. Whereas in India the reconstruction of traditions was an essential part of the national freedom movement, there was no such movement in Sri Lanka, which was granted independence as a matter of course once India was free. Sri Lanka had been granted the privilege of adult franchise as early as 1931, when India had still to be satisfied with a severely restricted franchise. But this had not led to a mobilisation of the masses in Sri Lanka due to the peculiar political form of its government. Instead of the British Parliament, it was the London County Council which had served as a model for Sri Lanka's legislature. This stabilised the kind of elite politics which characterised the political culture of the island even after the attainment of independence, when a regular parliament had replaced the old legislature. (de Silva 1986: 97-98) The elite communicated in English and there was as yet no sign of the cruel conflicts which tore Sri Lanka's body politic apart in subsequent years. But behind this harmonious facade Sinhalese and Tamil intellectuals had long since cultivated their separate search for a useful past. The Sinhalese were proud of their Buddhist traditions and the story of their origin in Northern India. The Jaffna Tamils had sharpened history as a weapon in their fight for equal rights with the Sinhalese. (Hellmann-Rajanayagam 1996) They claimed to reside in Sri Lanka at least as long as the Sinhalese if not even earlier. Once communal strife began, these weapons could be unsheathed and wielded with vigour.

The period immediately after the achievement of independence was dominated by the United National Party, which represented the old elite of colonial days. This elite was challenged by Solomon Bandaranaike and his Sri Lanka Freedom Party. Bandaranaike was himself a member of the landed Sinhala elite, but he had struck a different note even before independence. He wished to appeal to a broader social base and his allies were the "swabhasha educated", the young men trained in Buddhist monasteries. They hardly knew English and were therefore debarred from government service and the participation in elite politics. In 1956 Bandaranaike waged a successful election campaign, promising to make Sinhala the national language. He thus risked a direct confrontation with the Tamils as well as with those radical Buddhists whose aspirations he had encouraged but to whom he appeared not to go far enough. A radical Buddhist monk shot him in 1959. (de Silva 1986: 196-198) From now on the influential abbots of the Buddhist monasteries emerged as umpires in the political game.

After Bandaranaike's assassination the pendulum seemed to swing back to the UNP, but his widow Sirimavo soon won another election and continued her husband's political line. A particularly contentious issue was the introduction of quotas in colleges so as to reduce the chances of Tamil graduates in favour of the Sinhalese. The Tamils had opted much earlier for the British type of education and had captured a large part of the posts in government service. (de Silva 1986: 216-218) This imbalance was now to be redressed. On the face of it this seemed to be only fair. But the Tamils in their barren province had nothing to fall back upon while the Sinhalese who controlled the fertile South had earlier not even cared to compete for government posts. Young Tamils who had been denied career prospects easily drifted into terrorism and the Tamil Tiger, a powerful emblem ever since the days of the Tamil Chola dynasty which had once ruled parts of Sri Lanka, was pitted against the Sinhalese Lion.

Dividing the past and then the present and the future had also become Sri Lanka's unfortunate destiny. Sri Lanka's problems have not yet been resolved.

China: The end of empire and the rise of national communism

China has never been under colonial rule, but it was also fully exposed to the impact of European imperialism. In fact, the conditions imposed upon China served the imperial interests so well that there was no need to go in for the risky venture of occupying China. The Chinese intelligentsia knew this very well and deplored the weakness of their country which could only be cured if it also imbibed the strong Western medicine of nationalism. There was also a latent resentment against the ruling Qing dynasty which had obviously outlived the mandate of heaven and did nothing to improve China's position. In such periods of doubt one would always remember that this dynasty was actually not Chinese but Manchurian and thus alien to Chinese traditions. The Taiping rebellion almost brought about the collapse of the empire in the 1850s. (Gernet 1985: 545-547) It was put down with a heavy hand, but this did not necessarily strengthen the authority of the emperor but rather the authority of various warlords. A new vision was required and it was bound to follow the trend of "solidarity traditionalism", linking an assessment of China's current position with a recourse to reconstructed traditions and a vision of the future.

The most fascinating "solidarity traditionalist" who rose to prominence in late nineteenth century China was Kang Yu-wei (1858-1927). Whereas others who reconstructed traditions selected the appropriate ones and rejected those which did not fit into their scheme as later accretions, Kang Yu-wei adopted a more ingenious method: he identified a culprit who had falsified and misrepresented the tradition. This was the imperial librarian, Liu Hsin, who lived in the times of the early Han dynasty. After dealing with the culprit, Kang Yu-wei proceeded to portray Confucius, whose teachings had been twisted by Liu Hsin, as a democratic reformer whose thought was of immediate relevance to the present and the future. But Kang Yu-wei went even beyond this and outlined the features of a socialist utopia. However, this part of his work was not published in his life time. (Gernet 1985: 593-594) There is a similarity between his vision and Vivekananda's reconstruction of a socialist tradition mentioned above.

In propagating a reconstructed Confucianism Kang Yu-wei faced the same dilemma as other Chinese advocates of a "culturalist" approach to nationalism. Chinese traditional culture was universalist in its vision and did not easily fit in with defining China as one nation-state among many others. It also did not correspond to an ethnic definition of the nation as limited to the Han Chinese. It is perhaps for this reason that Kang Yu-wei finally turned to the new universalism of a socialist utopia. It may be mentioned in this context that in India Rabindranath Tagore emerged as an advocate of universalism as the essence of Indian tradition. He did not hesitate to condemn nationalism as a retrograde force, an assessment which was not popular with contemporary Indian nationalists.

Kang Yu-wei opted for nationalism rather than for universalism as far as his active participation in politics was concerned. At the end of the nineteenth century he was for a short time very influential as a reformer in Beijing, but when conservative circles proved to be more powerful he had to flee to Japan. The man who actually led the first Chinese revolution, Sun Yat-sen (1866-1925), was more a man of action than an inspiring thinker. He wished to unite nationalism and liberal democracy with a republican form of government. He was not a scholar and was also not imbued with Chinese tradition. He was inclined to opt for the ethnic approach to nationalism and wrote that race and state had been congruent in pre-modern China. But he was careful not to limit "race" to the Han Chinese as this would have alienated the members of Chinese ethnic minorities. Han-chauvinism would also not have corresponded to his cosmopolitan experience. He had spent much of his life abroad and had established a network of like-minded revolutionaries. But his success was mainly due to the fact that he was at the right place at the right time. (Gernet 1985: 625-626) The rule of the Qing dynasty ended in 1911 not with a bang but a whimper. He became President of the Republic of China proclaimed in Nanking, but knowing that discretion is the better part of valour, he transferred the presidency to the military dictator, Yuan Shikai, in Beijing who had actually no sympathies with Sun Yat-sen's democratic republicanism and restored the monarchy in 1916 with himself as the new emperor. He died a few months later and China was plunged into anarchy with various warlords dominating the different regions of the large country. Sun Yat-sen tried in vain to construct a republican political order, whereas his brother-in-law, Chiang Kai-shek, was more successful by playing the super-warlord and eliminating or subduing the others. (Gernet 1985: 630-631)

Whereas Sun Yat-sen was a rather shallow but sincere liberal republican, Chiang Kai-shek was the Chinese variant of a fascist and persecuted liberals and republicans. His authoritarian regime sponsored the New Life Movement which was supposed to give ideological respectability to his rule. Chiang was beaten at his game by the Japanese who invaded China with superior military force. As he could not stand up to them, he lost his appeal to the Chinese nation. His Communist enemies, whom he had failed to crush, were increasingly identified with the national cause.

As has been stated earlier, Marxists tend to regard nationalism as an instance of "false consciousness", thus it was strange that the Chinese communists easily absorbed nationalism without any ideological qualms. This was due to the fact that Marxist ideology when expressed in

Chinese terminology anyhow lost a great deal of the precision of "scientific socialism" and blended with traditional Chinese ideas. (Gernet 1985: 651-653) In this way it could also absorb nationalism in terms of a fervent anti-imperialist patriotism that had an appeal to many Chinese. Moreover, straightforward patriotism absolved them from opting either for "culturist" or "ethnic" nationalism as an ideology. However, the idea of liberal democracy was as much anathema to the Communists as to Chiang Kai-shek.

Nationalism from above: The case of Japan

Of all Asian nations, Japan seems to come closest to the ideal type of a nation: its island territory is very well defined, its population is fairly homogenous and it has a standardised and undisputed national language. Moreover, Japan was quite self-conscious about the debt it owed to Chinese civilisation. It felt the need to stress its indigenous merits so as to prove that its heritage was not a borrowed one. This mostly concerned scholars and not the common people, but these scholars were imbued with a kind of proto-nationalism. When Japan was threatened by the West it first tried to close its doors, but once these doors were pried open by military power, this proto-nationalism of the scholars was turned into an official nationalism which was imposed on the Japanese people from above. The Japanese emperor, the Tenno, played an important symbolic role in this official nationalism. Since Japan had the longest dynastic tradition in the world and the genealogy of the Tenno was traced to the sun goddess Amaterasu, he was a divine figure. Loyalty to the Tenno was a powerful element of the Japanese tradition and lend itself to a modern construction of nationalism.

The most important manifestation of national "traditionalist" thought was the so-called National School of Philosophy (*kokugaku*) which was active in the late eighteenth and the early nineteenth century. (Kracht 1990, Maruyama 1988: 36-38) Its main aim was to restore a pristine Shinto tradition from which the foreign influences of Confucianism and Buddhism were to be removed. This implied an attack on all theories and ideologies and a praise of intuition as a specifically Japanese approach to life and thought. The problem with this type of philosophy was that its lacked any doctrine which could be taught to others. In order to tackle this problem a leading light of this school, Hirata Atsutane (1776-1843), adopted a syncretist line and combined Confucian and Buddhist ideas so as to produce a special Japanese philosophy. (Maruyama 1988: 37) His ideas are very similar to those of other Asian "solidarity traditionalists". A younger contemporary of Hirata, Aisawa Seishisai (1781-1863) then hit upon a convenient term which expressed the trend of thought of the national philosophers: *kokutai* which can be freely translated as the body of the country. It seems that this term was first mentioned in Aisawa's book *Shinron* written in 1825 and later on gained currency among nationalists. (Maruyama 1988: 45-46) It corresponded to the intuitive tendency of *kokagaku*. It could not be clearly defined but had a quasi-magical quality. Thus it became soon closely associated with the Tenno and his divine origin. Loyalty to him and to the nation could be blended in this way. The noblemen (*samurai*) who supported the Meiji-Restauration, i.e. the elimination of the Shogun and the re-instatement of the Tenno as supreme authority, were deeply imbued with such ideas. This nationalism from above also found an eloquent expression in the Tenno's edict on education of 1890. (Maruyama 1988: 45-46) This edict was far more than an administrative document, it could be called a national manifesto. It projected the idea of a corporate national state based on the loyalty to the Tenno. Education was meant to inculcate social solidarity rather than individualism.

Kokutai lent itself to totalitarian interpretations. Its vague meaning could be made to fit into various ideological constructs, including fascism and militarism. The attraction of such extreme variants of nationalism was demonstrated by the surprising career of Kita Ikki (1883-1937) (Wilson 1969, Shillony 1988). He started out as a socialist and was a virulent critic of the Tenno system. He then participated in the Chinese revolution of 1911 and preached the ideology of "Asianism" which was in vogue at that time. He became a convert to Nichiren-Buddhism, and on his return to Japan he published in 1919 a plan for the reconstruction of Japan. In this he already advocated a military coup. He then backed the officers who staged the coup of 1936 and was executed in 1937. His life showed both the intellectual confusion prevailing in Japan and the desire for a commitment to the cause of nationalism in its most extreme form.

Another problem associated with the concept of *kokutai* is its static rather than dynamic character. It is perennial and thus cannot change in the course of time. But there was a supplementary concept, that of *bunmei* (civilisation) which was interpreted by its principal advocate, Fukuzawa Yukichi, in terms of a sequence of stages of cultural development which would also apply to Japan. He may have been influenced by evolutionists like Herbert Spencer. Obviously Fukuzawa was careful enough not to extend his stages of development so as to cover the political sphere, otherwise he could have faced the problem of discussing monarchy as a stage of political development.

As mentioned earlier the reconstruction of traditions in the interest of nationalism depended on the elements of tradition available for such an exercise. In Japan the Tenno proved to be such an element. The traditional allegiance to him was brought into an entirely new focus under the auspices of nationalism. The anxiety of the Japanese that the Tenno might have to abdicate after losing the Second World War was due to the feeling that *kokutai* could vanish if it was no longer supported by the loyalty to the Tenno.

Concluding remarks

This highly selective survey of Asian nations reflects the greater familiarity of the author with South Asia and the fact that his knowledge of developments in China and Japan is rather limited. He has turned to them only in order to acquire a comparative perspective. He has completely omitted the varied spectrum of Southeast Asian nations. The aim of this survey was not an encyclopaedic coverage but an attempt at illustrating some basic features of the reconstruction of tradition in the interest of nationalism that seem to be of universal importance. Referring once more to the Polish case mentioned in the beginning it can be stated that the denial of national self-determination and the humiliation by imperial powers is of great importance for the rise of nationalism. As far as the reconstruction of traditions that help to justify nationalism is concerned, it has been shown that for obvious reasons those traditions that support solidarity are given preference. It has also been shown that the quest for a useful past may not always lead to a unified past but can also end in its irreparable division.

References:

Anderson, Benedict (1991), *Imagined Communities. Reflections on the Spread and Origin of Nationalism*, New York

Dalberg-Acton, Lord John 1967 (orig.1862), "Nationality", in: William McNeill, ed., *Essays in the Liberal Interpretation of History. Selected Papers of Lord Acton*, Chicago

de Silva, Kingsley M. (1986), *Managing Ethnic Tensions in Multi-ethnic Societies. Sri Lanka 1880-1985*, Lanham

Deutsch, Karl W. (1966), *Nationalism and Social Communication*, Cambridge (Mass.)

Dittmer, Kerrin (1972), *Die indischen Muslims und die Hindi-Urdu Kontroverse in den United Provinces*, Wiesbaden

Gellner, Ernest (1994), *Encounters with Nationalism*, Oxford

Gernet, Jacques (1985), *A History of Chinese Civilization*, Cambridge

Hellmann-Rajanayagam, Dagmar (1996), "Die Jaffna-Tamilen und ihre Geschichte", in: *Periplus. Jahrbuch für Außereuropäische Geschichte 1996*, Münster

Kaviraj, Sudipata (1992), "Writing, Speaking, Beimg. Languages and the Historical Formation of Identities in India", in: Dagmar Hellmann-Rajanayagam/Dietmar Rothermund (eds.), *Nationalstaat und Sprachkonflikte in Süd- und Südostasien,* Stuttgart

Kracht, K. (1990), "Nationale Philosophie", in: Horst Hammitzsch (ed.), *Japan Handbuch*, Stuttgart

Maruyama, Masao (1988), *Denken in Japan,* (trsl. by W. Schamoni and W. Seifert), Frankfurt

Rothermund, Dietmar (1965), *Die politische Willensbildung in Indien, 1900-1960*, Wiesbaden

Rothermund, Dietmar (1970), "Traditionalism and Socialism in Vivekananda's Thought", in: *Quest* No.67/ 1970, pp.34 ff. , reprinted in Dietmar Rothermund (1970), *The Phases of Indian Nationalism and other essays*, Bombay

Rothermund, Dietmar (1979), "Traditionalism and National Solidarity in India", in: Robin Moore (ed.), *Tradition and Politics in South Asia,* New Delhi

Rothermund, Dietmar (1989), *Mahatma Gandhi. Der Revolutionär der Gewaltlosigkeit: eine politische Biographie,* München

Rothermund, Dietmar (1998), *Mahatma Gandhi. An essay in political biography*, New Delhi

Roy, Anuradha (1995), "Foreign Tyrants or Foster Brothers? Muslims in the eyes of Hindu nationalists in nineteenth century Bengal", in: *The Calcutta Historical Journal*, Vol. XVII, No.1 (Jan.-June 1995) pp.123 ff.

Shillony, Ben-Ami (1988), "Kita Ikki", in: A. Embree (ed.), *Encyclopedia of Asian History,* New York: Asia Society, Vol.2,p. 321 f.

Stokes, Eric (1978), *The Peasant and the Raj. Studies in*

agrarian society and peasant rebellion in colonial India, Cambridge

Wilson, George M. (1969), *Radical Nationalist in Japan: Kitta Ikki 1883-1937*, Cambridge

Wolpert, Stanley (1984), *Jinnah of Pakistan*, New York/Oxford

---

I wish to thank my colleagues at Heidelberg University, Professors Susanne Weigelin-Schwiedrzik (Chinese Studies) and Wolfgang Seifert (Japanese Studies) with whom I conducted a joint seminar in the summer term of 1993 on traditionalism in India, China and Japan. This comparative study greatly contributed to the development of the ideas outlined in this article.

Nation and Region in Indian Historiography

Modern historiography in India was stimulated by nationalism. In fact, the concepts of historiography as a specific scholarly discipline and of nationalism as an ideology reached India more or less at the same time in the 19th century and gave rise to a powerful blend of nationalist scholarship in history. Of course, India was not devoid of historiography in earlier times and the Indian term *itihas* refers to narratives of the past in much the same way as Western terms (history, Geschichte etc.). But earlier Indian historiography was primarily regional as exemplified by Kalhana's *Rajatarangini*, a chronicle of medieval Kashmir. Kalhana shows a great deal of awareness of other Indian regions, particularly when he reports on Lalitaditya's famous tour of conquest which followed the East coast down to the South and back to Kashmir via Western India and Afghanistan. But Kalhana's focus is definitely regional. This is also true of a hitherto neglected type of Indian historiography, the introductions (*prashasti*) of innumerable land grant documents on copper tablets. These introductions are devoted to the praise of the king who made the grant and of his ancestors who contributed to the grandeur of the dynasty. These texts throw much light on the regional history of medieval India. The increasing attention which has been devoted to regional history in recent years will lead to a more detailed exploration of such sources. For nationalist historians the evidence of regional diversity was a disturbing feature. They took pride in ancient empires which could be interpreted as harbingers of national glory and had no use for regional kingdoms. They were anxious to find traces of the concept of an Indian nation in the past and could not find them in earlier Indian historiography.

Historicity and National Destiny

It was not only the concept of an Indian nation which was absent from earlier Indian historiography, it also lacked the peculiar sense of historicity which was so characteristic of modern Western historiography. Actually the often repeated Western judgement that India had no "sense of history" was a striking testimony to Western ignorance of the historical conditions which had led to the fairly recent emergence of such a "sense" in Europe itself. The Western mode of consciousness had changed from one which placed man above history into one which emphasized the total historicity of man and this had happened only in the late 18th century. Man above history was independent of the historical process, he could reflect on it, derive lessons from it or neglect it, but he did not think of himself as a historical product, totally bound up within history. It must be stressed that this modern mode of consciousness may not at all be the final one. Michel Foucault has argued that it may disappear as quickly as it rose to prominence. Therefore Indian minds which have resisted this mode of consciousness may be in a way ahead of their times rather than lagging behind.

Mahatma Gandhi's attitude towards history is a case in point. He wrote in 1924 after having read the great Indian epic *Mahabharata* in prison: "I believe in the saying that a nation is happy that has no history. It is my pet theory that our Hindu ancestors solved the question for us by ignoring history as it is understood today and by building on slight events their philosophical structure. Such is the Mahabharata. The immortal but unknown author of the Mahabharata weaves into his story sufficient of the supernatural to warn you against taking him literally. (Modern Western historians)... are unnecessarily at pains to tell you they are giving you facts and nothing but facts. Names and forms matter little, they come and go. That which is permanent and therefore necessary eludes the historian of events. Truth transcends history."

Modern Indian historians did not subscribe to Gandhi's "pet theory", on the contrary they tried to do their best in emulating the standards set by Western historiography. Instead of believing that a nation is happy that has no history, they reconstructed a national history for India. Even works which appeared to be contributions to regional history like Rajendralal Mitra's famous "Antiquities of Orissa" were written from a national point of view. Mitra wanted to prove that India had developed a style of art and architecture on her own and thus combat the views of European historians who attributed everything in this field in India to Greek influence. Similarly R.C. Majumdar's "Ancient Indian Colonies in the Far East" was a nationalist historian's contribution to the glorification of "Greater India". If the British could lay claim to being the greatest colonial power in modern times, India could point to the same kind of achievements in the past. It was a bold vision of national destiny which inspired this type of historiography.

The "quest for a useful past" was, of course, most promising if one turned to the glories of ancient India. The more recent past was not very attractive, in fact, it was deliberately painted in dark colours by nationalist historians who had to explain why India had lost her freedom. British superiority was anyhow celebrated by British historians and Indian nationalist historians naturally did not want to join that chorus. By contrast they had to deplore the national degradation which was India's sad fate in the eighteenth century in order to explain why India had succumbed to foreign rule. Due to this tendency the eighteenth century acquired such a bad reputation that only very few Indian scholars of earlier generations took a closer look at it at all. This has changed only in recent years as regional studies have shown that there was a great deal of political and commercial vitality in India at that time. Moreover, even those regions of India which came under colonial rule in the eighteenth century were not as easily penetrated by the British as earlier historians had thought.

The Dangers of Traditionalism and Communalism

The nationalist quest for a useful past led to the inherent danger of emphasizing a particular type of solidarity traditionalism, i.e. a selective reconstruction of tradition which would enhance national solidarity. Religious traditions inevitably played a prominent role in this respect. There was also a practical aspect with regard to the access to historical sources: Hindu historians were naturally more familiar with Sanskrit sources relating to ancient Indian history and Muslim historians were attached to their Persian sources which provided information about a later period of Indian history. This led to a strange coincidence of opposites: Historians of these two types would agree that there was a clearly demarcated Hindu period of Indian history followed by an equally distinctive Muslim period and finally a British period in which both Hindus and Muslims were subjected to foreign rule. Some of the more communal-minded Hindu historians would even argue that Muslim rule was already foreign rule and that the Hindu nation had lost its independence long ago. Instances of Hindu resistance to Muslim rule could then be interpreted as proto -nationalist movements. This tendency could occasionally inspire detailed work in regional history such as the history of Maharashtra under Shivaji who was projected as a major national figure although he was a regional ruler. Later on regional historical research was also stimulated by the various state committees entrusted with collecting material concerning the history of the freedom movement. Again the motive was a national one, but the subject directed attention to regional history.

The Impact of Historical Materialism

After independence nationalist historiography was eclipsed for various reasons. First of all, the challenge of foreign rule which had provided such a strong motive for it was no longer there. Contracts for writing up the history of the freedom movement were some incentive, but in a way this enterprise was a rearguard action of nationalist historiography. There was a lack of enthusiasm for this kind of command performance. This may also explain why the great "Towards Freedom"- Project which was supposed to parallel the massive British publication of documents relating to "The Transfer of Power" was delayed for a long time. No major Indian historian was ready to devote himself entirely to this kind of work. Finally a sensible method of farming out this work was adopted, a senior historian acted as the general editor and others were commissioned to edit volumes each of which would cover one year. In this way some progress has been made in this line in recent years – though rather belated, indeed.

The new trend in Indian historiography which contributed to the eclipse of nationalist historiography was the strong impact which historical materialism had on the younger generation of historians. The modern mode of consciousness which emphasized the historicity of man has been mentioned before. This mode found its most convincing and radical expression in historical materialism, because Marx did not just stress historicity in general but outlined in detail the forces which condition the process of human development. Marxist historians thus emerged as truly modern historians. Unfortunately Marx had invented the strange category of the "Asiatic mode of production" with which he exempted Asia from the "normal" dynamics of human development. But Indian Marxist historians accepted this as a challenge and tried to prove that Indian history had also taken the "normal" course prescribed by Marx. This motivated them to do a great deal of regional historical research, because modes of production have to be analysed at the local and regional base and not at the national apex. This does not mean that Indian Marxist historians did not take an interest in national history as they saw it. They could find a common denominator with nationalist historians in terms of anti-imperialism. Thus, they could appreciate economic nationalism as a form on anti-imperialism. But in general the interests of nationalist and Marxist historians diverged.

The emphasis on regional social and economic history stimulated Indian historiography very much. The new generation of Marxist historians introduced many important themes and encouraged thorough and analytical scholarship whereas the nationalist historians seemed to rehash only old themes. However, the institutional support for historical scholarship also showed important regional variations. Bengal had been a stronghold of nationalist historiography and then emerged as the centre of Marxist historiography. Delhi, the national capital with its major universities also supported a great deal of historical research and experienced the same change of guards from nationalist to Marxist historians. But regional centres elsewhere lagged behind, because they never had such strong history departments. Nevertheless, some bright scholars emerged also in the "diaspora" and set new standards of historical research. In this way regional history has advanced in India in recent years. National history has been somewhat neglected in this way and one could only hope for its revival – not as nationalist history, but as a new type of history which draws strength from the advances in regional history.

History from Below: The message of "Subaltern Studies"

A new venture in Indian historiography appeared in 1982 when the first volume of "Subaltern Studies" was published – to be followed by several volumes in subsequent years. With these volumes the terminology of Antonio Gramsci entered into the discourse of Indian historians. "Subaltern" and "hegemony" soon became watchwords familiar to all younger historians. Gramsci had coined these terms when trying to analyse his own Italian society in which the working class was still rather marginal and civil servants of all kinds rather than capitalists represented the dominant strata. These strata established a social and cultural hegemony which enabled them to keep the "subaltern" groups in their place. Gramsci's version of historical materialism seemed to fit the Indian experience better than the class categories of Marx. At the same time the rather flexible term "subaltern" easily provided a challenge to "elitist historiography" and could accommodate a wide spectrum of narratives concerning local protest movements, peasant consciousness, etc. The volumes of "Subaltern Studies" are replete with such narratives, but very few of them actually fit in with the frame of reference established by Gramsci. Nevertheless, they all contribute in some way or the other to an awareness of "history from below". In keeping with this they have concentrated on local and regional history and some of them have been of seminal importance in this respect.

Caste and Indian Historiography

These advances in regional history may also fill a remarkable gap in Indian historiography: the history of caste as a social phenomenon. Studies of this subject are conspicuous by their absence in the field of historical research whereas they abound in anthropological literature. Historians seem to have been glad to leave this subject to the anthropologists. But there is more to this than a reluctance to transcend disciplinary boundaries. Both major trends in Indian historiography, the nationalist and the Marxist ones, were averse to a study of caste as a historical phenomenon. For the nationalist historian caste appeared to be the most fundamental challenge to national solidarity. Apologetic explanations of the "caste system" would only make matters worse. Moreover, the "caste (*varna*) system" as a nationwide phenomenon was of a highly abstract nature. The four major castes (brahmin, kshatriya, vaishya, shudra = priest, warrior, merchant, peasant) were delineated as such in the normative writings of the brahmins. Historians were sceptical about treating normative prescriptions as descriptions of historical facts. Anthropologists on the other hand were glad to encounter a society which had produced social categories of its own which could be readily used by them. Due to the special nature of their discipline anthropologists strive for systematic explanations, but are also very sensitive with regard to the imposition of alien categories on the cultures which they observe. India was thus an ideal case for them and Indian anthropologists trained by Western anthropologists readily adopted the same point of view. Indian historians, however, resented what they considered to be a Western obsession with caste in India. Therefore nationalist historians refrained from using caste as an analytical category, and Marxist historians did the same, although for different reasons.

The fundamental exercise for a Marxist historian is class analysis, and caste and class are incompatible social categories. Low caste status correlates to some extent with a low economic position, but high caste status does not necessarily imply wealth and economic power. Brahmin capitalists are very rare, indeed. Therefore Marxist historians neglected caste and rather concentrated on economic stratification. In this way caste became a subject which was obviously not worth the historian's attention. This also prevented the historians from looking at caste (*jati*) as a regional phenomenon and exploring features of Indian society which would certainly have been worth their attention.

Indian society in its regional manifestation may be termed a sedimentary one. Just like the geologist who identifies several layers of sediments, the historian can identify different social layers in Indian regions which defined themselves or where defined by others as castes (*jati*). Some of them emerged from tribesmen who became peasants, some from conquerors who imposed themselves on the respective regional society, some came as itinerant cultural experts (brahmins) who were either looking for patronage or were invited by those who were interested in their services. Until they hardened in the course of time, these layers were often quite fluid and the normative projection of a hierarchical "system" did not at all reflect social reality. Recently a young Indian historian has tried to identify references to castes in the medieval inscriptions of Orissa. This pioneering work throws much light on the fluidity of caste formation in that region. It is to be hoped that this work will be parallelled elsewhere in India. Some of the contributors to "Subaltern Studies" have also provided new insights into the actual observance of caste distinctions at the local level. In this way the old prejudices of nationalist and Marxist historians which reinforced each other in this respect may be overcome by a younger generation of historians.

Modern Indian Historians – an Isolated Sub-culture of Experts?

One fundamental problem must be mentioned here at the end of this very brief survey of the main trends of Indian historiography: the discrepancy of the modes of consciousness. Many Indians – whether they otherwise agree with him or not – would probably share Mahatma Gandhi's view of history and not the so called "modern" view which (for reasons stated above) is most strongly represented in India by Marxist historians. To that extent "modern" Indian historians represent what Habermas would call an isolated sub-culture of experts. They operate on the same wavelength among themselves and with sympathetic colleagues abroad, but may be out of touch with their own people, at least with regard to their professional work.

For the Marxist historians the recent collapse of the socialist world system is a special predicament. This collapse certainly does not invalidate historical materialism as a method of analysis as such, but it does deprive the Marxists of a vision which was so closely bound up with the mode of consciousness which attributed a specific meaning to the historicity of man. The nationalist historians lost a great deal of their impetus after the attainment of independence as the freedom struggle was over in which nationalist historiography had played an important role. Marxist historians nowadays face a similar problem, not because their dreams have come true but because their visions are no longer what they used to be. Dreams come true and disappointed visions may be equally demotivating for historians, they may then simply continue their disciplinary routine and as long as there are institutions which will support them they are going to survive – as an isolated sub-culture of experts.

Is there a new vision which could inspire historians in India as well as elsewhere? It may be the idea of a history of mankind and this history cannot be studied in the abstract but only in its regional manifestations. The delimitation of the region may vary in accordance with the issue concerned, it may be a continent, a country, a particular area or even a village. India encompasses about one fifth of mankind and many regions with a rich history of their own. Seen from this perspective it is a paradise for historians, and if those who are already there can convey this idea to their countrymen and to the rest of mankind they will not remain an isolated sub-culture of experts.

INDEX

Note: The following words have not been included in the index: British, India, politics, South Asia, state. They occur so often in the text that almost every other page would have had to be listed here. The names of authors whose publications have been cited in the text (Harvard style) are printed in italics in the index.